THE JUMBO BOOK OF FUNNY JOKES FOR KIDS

1000+ JOKES

RIDDLELAND

Table of Contents

Riddleland Bonus

Join our **Facebook Group** at **Riddleland for Kids**
to get daily jokes and riddles.

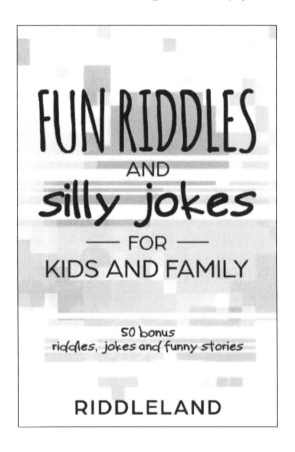

https://pixelfy.me/riddlelandbonus

Thank you for buying this book. As a token of our appreciation,
we would like to offer a special bonus—a collection
of 50 original jokes, riddles, and funny stories.

Introduction

Welcome to one of the best joke books in the world - if not the very best.

We love joke books, and growing up, we have read a lot of joke books. One of the problems with most of the joke books we've read is that they have the same jokes as the other joke books. We know you have been there too.

That is why we set off on an adventure to uncover 1000+ jokes that you likely have not heard before. Trust us, we left no stone unturned!

Our goal is to be fresh and different – and funny! We've crafted question-and answer jokes, puns, silly scenarios, knock-knock jokes, one-liners, and riddles and have grouped them by subject. We got everything from animals, barbers, birthdays, cars, computers, pirates, outer space, and numerous other topics that will tickle your funny bones. Can you think of any other joke book that has almost everything, including the kitchen sink?

This book has over 1000 jokes. Every joke is so squeaky clean, you can share it with your grandma without a hint of embarrassment of fear of soap coming your way. a bar of soap.

Whether you are reading this book aloud to a friend, giggling to yourself on the bus, or memorizing a few lines for family talent night, we hope these jokes lift your spirits and put a smile on your face. Don't forget to let us know what you think when you're done; there's a feedback card in the back of the book just waiting for your thoughts.

Chapter One:
Animals

Some animals are cute and cuddly. Others are brutes. All can be funny. Here are some animal jokes to get us started.

Why was the pelican out of money?

He had a big bill.

How many cockroaches does it take to change a lightbulb?

Nobody knows; as soon as the bulb comes on, they all scatter.

How are geese flying South similar to a dictionary being thrown?

Both are flying in formation.

Animals

Why did the dog avoid standing on the American scale?

He had been brought up to fear dog pounds.

Which animal would have complained if it wasn't mentioned first in this book?

The skunk would have made a big stink.

How is an airplane safety device similar to a slide for parrots?

One is a parachute, and the other is a parrot chute.

When is a good time to learn something about dogs?

When you need to pick up a few pointers.

How is a dog's tail similar to the story Little Red Riding Hood?

Both are furry tails.

What animal is the tallest?

The caterpillar has 100 feet.

What is so bad about having 144 female sheep?

It's ewe, gross!

Is accuracy needed in describing
how many times a dog barks
in an hour?

No. Most people are okay with
ruff estimates.

Why couldn't the pet shop
have a Dalmatian?

The janitor kept the place
spotless.

How is a goat similar
to margarine?

Both can work as butters.

Why did the bull play
his stereo so loudly?

He wanted to be a heard animal.

What did the owl in the Santa
hat say?

"Hoo! Hoo! Hoo!"

What do you call people who
are shocked to learn there are mammals
other than humans who know how
to swim?

People who are in otter disbelief.

Why do most people seem amazed
when a dog shakes hands
with them?

The dog gives them pause.

What type of otter wears
eyeglasses?

The see otter.

What do you call an otter
with rare habits?

An odder.

Why is the crow charity named
"Caw, Caw, Caw, Caw".

It's four good caws.

Which animal exaggerates a lot?

The giraffe;
Giraffes tell tall tales.

What animal will take vehicles without
permission?

Common deer.

Animals

What do you call a lion with chicken pox?

The dotted lion.

Do you believe me when I tell you I saw a dog with a six-foot tail?

I admit it's a tall tail.

Which animal carries around spare change?

The skunk has cents.

What's the name of the do-it-yourself moving company that transports sheep?

Ewe-Haul

What kind of terriers are kept inside?

Interiors.

Which bee is the most modest?

The humble bee.

What do you call a baby bird that writes stories?

A fledgling author.

What musical instrument do chickens play?

Drums; you've probably heard of their drumsticks.

What kind of dog does King Midas have?

A golden retriever.

Why don't rhinoceroses wear deodorant?

They don't want to become ex-stink.

How can you identify a bald eagle?

The feathers on its scalp are all combed over to one side.

What animal is required to be with you if you arrest a monk and put him in prison?

The monk key.

Where did the gossiping farmer lead his cattle so he could hear the latest rumors?

He herded through the grapevine.

How is a sad girl like a boy touching a goose feather?

Both are feeling down.

Animals

What kind of creative ideas do snakes get?

New fang-led ones.

What happened after the horse ate four quarters?

It bucked.

What birds like to gossip?

Owls. They are always asking, "Who? Who?"

Why was the cook called to make peace between the two warring chickens?

He had a can of chick peace.

How is fresh bread like a bitter female deer?

Both are sour doe.

Which insect did the poet write his poem on?

The poet said he wrote his latest poem on the fly.

Which member of the sheep family gets pranked?

The joke's often on ewe.

How did a father bird excuse his son's pranks?

"He's a chirp off the ol' block."

Which bird tends to brag?

The crow.

How are two containers of Coke like two tropical birds?

The first is two cans and the second is toucans.

How is a bargain different from a canary?

One is cheap and the other is a little cheeper.

The teacher was helping children learn the plural forms of animals.
For instance, when she asked, "What do you call it if you have more than one cow?"
The class answered, "Cows".

She then asked, "What do you call more than one goose?"
The class yelled in unison, "Geese."

Seeing the class was on a roll, she asked, "What do you call more than one mouse?"
"Mice."

The teacher continued questioning, "What do you call if there's more than one spider?"
"Help!"

Two young witches were talking to each other.

The first said, "Last night I shouted the magic words that I thought would turn me into a pony."

Her friend looked at her curiously and asked, "Did it work?"

"No, but I didn't give up. I kept shouting them. Over and over! Again and again."

"Did the spell finally work?"

"Sort of. Today I'm a little hoarse."

Animals

Try These Tongue Twisters

Two tired turtles turned to tour two tires two times Tuesday.

You better believe Bobo the Bull bit the bullet
by biting bites bit by bit.

Dad's dog, Dog, dogged Dale during Dale's daily drive
down the dreary dale.

Knock-Knock.

Who's there?
Silly Bulls.

Silly Bulls who?
**Silly Bulls are units of pronunciation;
for instance, "water" - "wa" "ter" - has
two syllables.**

Knock-Knock.

Who's there?
Hyper Lynx.

Hyper Lynx who?
**Hyper Lynx are what take you from
one website to another website on the
Internet.**

Knock-Knock.

Who's there?
My Crow.

My Crow who?
**My Crow scope will let you see
microorganisms.**

Knock-Knock.

Who's there?
Locusts.

Locusts who?
**Locusts (low costs) are how businesses
attract customers.**

Knock-Knock.

Who's there?
Worm.

Worm who?
Worm in here, isn't it; or are you a little chilly.

Knock-Knock.

Who's there?
My Newt.

My Newt who?
My Newt (minute) and tiny ants are often overlooked.

Knock-Knock.

Who's there?
Bay Bee.

Bay Bee who?
Bay Bee cried all night; no one could sleep.

Knock-Knock.

Who's there?
Goose.

Goose who?
Goose who has more knock-knock jokes for you.

Knock-Knock.

Who's there?
Eel.

Eel who?
Eel figure it out; don't you worry.

Knock-Knock.

Who's there?
Ox.

Ox who?
Ox me for another knock-knock joke.

Chapter Two:
Automobiles

I don't know about you, but I like to go on car rides. I like sticking my head out the window and waving to my friends. I find every part of life to be funny – and car rides are no exception. Here are some automobile jokes that will take us down the road of laughter.

Why did the filling station attendant go to the doctor?

He had a lot of gas.

Was the tire excited about the upcoming car ride?

It was pumped.

Why didn't the driver of the electric car park on the cul-de-sac?

There was no outlet.

Why did the nervous car
go to the doctor?

He felt like a wreck.

What kind of reptiles
drive cars?

Tail gators.

Why did the man insist on standing
in the middle of the highway to sign
the contract?

He had been told to sign on
the dotted line.

When do people prank gas
station attendants?

On April Fuels Day.

What do you call over-priced tires?

Highway rubbery.

How are many religious people like
racing car drivers?

They both like to go fast.

What type of dogs enjoy
watching auto racing?

Lap dogs.

What did one flower say to the other
flower when it wanted
to go faster in the sportscar?

"Put the petal to the metal."

What do most new cars have that
most babies require?

A rear wiper.

Why did the driving instructor
go to the baseball game?

He wanted to see a line drive
and a baseball park.

Why did the auto mechanic who worked
on recreational vehicles (RVs) get
recruited by the baseball team?

He knew how to make a home run.

What happened when the car's
engine got mad?

It blew a gasket.

Automobiles

Why has the price of tires increased so much?

Inflation.

Why does Tarzan swing on a vine?

He can't drive a stick.

How did the driver prove his claim that he was the car's best handler?

He backed it up.

Why did the stop light turn red?

It saw the stoplight down the street changing.

What did the icy road say to the car?

"Want to go for a spin?"

Why did the squirrel watch the auto mechanic so intently?

He wanted to see how the car was held together with bolts . . . and nuts.

How do you describe someone who is half-listening to a conversation about 18-wheelers?

Semi-interested.

Why should you not use
a plastic discount card to scrape off
ice from your windshield?

You usually only get 10-25% off with
a discount card.

What inspires a mechanic?

He has auto motives.

Why was the mechanic so tired after
working on the tailpipe?

It was exhausting work.

Why can't you trust what
a car's heater tells you?

Because heaters blow hot air.

Why did the boy go to the school
counselor about the car stereo speaker?

He wanted sound advice.

What fuel powers
clown cars?

Laughing gas.

What do you call a car
covered in fallen leaves?

An autumn-mobile.

Which animal enjoys car rides?

Spiders like to go for a spin.

How do you know a car
is thinking?

You can see its wheels turning.

Why didn't the police arrest
the dead car battery?

They couldn't find anything
to charge it with.

Why was the banana pulled over
by the police while driving his car?

He peeled out.

What do an old car, a new baby,
and a poisonous snake have
in common?

A rattle.

Automobiles

What happened when the ice-cream truck turned over?

The road was covered with cones.

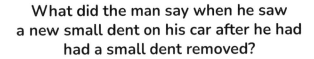

What part of being a mechanic did the former explosive expert like best?

Blowing up the tires.

What did the man say when he saw a new small dent on his car after he had had a small dent removed?

"If it's not one ding, it's another?"

Why was the engine humming?

It didn't know the words.

Why was the U-Haul driver crying?

It was a moving experience.

Why don't you ever see any babies as auto mechanics?

They lack motor skills.

What sound did the honeybee make when it was struck by the car's windshield?

Bee flat.

How can you tell a car from a goat?

Cars have one horn; goats have two horns.

What's the first step for learning how to be a mechanic?

Buy a starter kit.

What do the butcher and the car thief have in common?

Both work at chop shops.

What is the race car driver's favorite meal of the day?

Brake fast.

Why did the driver in front of the goose's car get upset with the goose at the red stoplight?

The goose wouldn't stop honking.

What type of water can steer a car?

Driving rain.

Why don't things ever go smoothly for the tow truck driver?

There's always a hitch.

Automobiles

What is a car's favorite dance?

The brake dance.

What is the smartest part of a car?

The headlights; they are very bright.

What happened to the man who had a fear of speed bumps?

He slowly got over it.

What does an otter drive?

An otter-mobile.

What kind of jokes do car engines prefer?

Knock-Knock jokes.

Customer: Do you hear that whistling coming from the front tire?

Mechanic: I do. It sounds like a flat.

Customer: A flat? Are you a musician too?

A mechanic was driving home from the auto garage
one day when a flying saucer landed on the road in front of him.
Curious as to what had landed, the mechanic got out of his car.

As he got closer, the hatch of the flying saucer opened and an alien stepped out,
pointing a ray gun at the mechanic.

The mechanic was unphased and kept walking toward
the flying saucer; the alien called,
"Stop. I am a UFO. Do you know what that stands for?"

"Of course," said the mechanic. "My vehicle is one too."

The alien looked at him suspiciously. "I don't think you are,"

he sneered. "I am too. It says so right above the gas cap -
Unleaded Fuel Only."

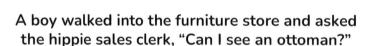

A boy walked into the furniture store and asked
the hippie sales clerk, "Can I see an ottoman?"

"You'll have to go down to the local garage and
ask the mechanic, man."

Sign seen in an auto garage:
Good, quick, cheap – pick any two.

A man carried a piece of asphalt into the restaurant
with him and placed it in the booth beside him.

When the waitress came to take his order,
he said, "I'd like a cup of coffee and one for the road, please."

Automobiles

Some people name their cars.

My friend even named the slots on the air conditioning dial;
he calls them "Hy", "Norm", and "Max".

"Let's see how much you know about driving,"
one friend said to another.
"What does the yellow light on a stoplight mean?"

"Slow down."

"Okay.
Wha—a-a-a-a-at does the
yel-l-l-l-l-low l-l-l-l-light
on a s-s-s-s-s-sstop l-l-l-l-l-l-light
me-e-e-e-e-ean?"

A man was car shopping with a salesman. The man found a car
he liked and looked over the front and insides of the car.

"Cargo room?" he asked.

The salesman replied, "Car go v-v-v-v-room v-v-v-v-vroom."

Inventor: I have just created a car that runs on pigpower
instead of horsepower.

Mechanic: Is pigpower better?

Inventor: Yes, except for one thing.

Mechanic: What's that?

Inventor: The tires squeal.

Try These Tongue Twisters

Karen was caring while carrying a carload cargo of crisp, cut carrots.

Carlos could care less about careless, costly car care.

Carl's Car Lot carries lots of custom cars for Carl's car customers' convenience.

Amy's auto ought to auto-start out of automatic parking gear.

Knock-Knock.

Who's there?
Auto Body.

Auto Body who?
Auto Body experiences are weird; people say you can see your body as you look down on it.

Knock-Knock.

Who's there?
Fueled.

Fueled who?
Fueled you, didn't I? You didn't recognize me.

Knock-Knock.

Who's there?
Car Ma.

Car Ma who?
Car Ma is the universe giving you what you deserve.

Knock-Knock.

Who's there?
Otto.

Otto who?
Otto-matic transmission comes standard in most cars.

Automobiles

Knock-Knock.

Who's there?
Phil R. Upp.

Phil R. Upp who?
Phil R. Upp; I'd like the tank full of gas please.

Knock-Knock.

Who's there?
Cool Aunt.

Cool Aunt who?
Cool Aunt is used to keep the radiator from overheating.

Knock-Knock.

Who's there?
Four Wheel.

Four Wheel who?
**Four Wheel, I am not kidding; it is really fun
telling jokes.**

Knock-Knock.

Who's there?
Myles A. Head.

Myles A. Head who?
Myles A. Head (kilometers ahead for those using the metric system) we will find a filling station.

Knock-Knock.

Who's there?
Lisa Ford.

Lisa Ford who?
Lisa Ford; lease a Honda; lease a Chevy; leasing lets you rent a car rather than buy it.

Knock-Knock.

Who's there?
Wheel.

Wheel who?
Wheel be able to finish this book tonight if we keep reading.

Knock-Knock.

Who's there?
Lane.

Lane who?
Lane (laying) down to go to sleep.

Knock-Knock.

Who's there?
Avenue.

Avenue who?
Avenue any more knock-knock jokes?

Chapter Three:
Birthdays

Everybody has one every year – a birthday!

Whether you celebrate your completion of another trip around the sun with cake, ice cream, presents, friends, and family, or simply reflect on the past year, I hope all your birthdays are happy days.

Some people hate growing older; other people love it. Really young people and really old people tend to count the months as well as the years – a toddler is proud to be "1 ½" and a senior adult brags about being "98 1/2", but most of us just count the number of years. Whether you like growing older or not, you're likely to enjoy this birthday humor.

Is age just a number?

No. I think "age" is a word.

Why are people hard to recognize when they stop being three years old?

Because we have never seen them be four (before).

What did the birthday cake coo to the knife?

"Aren't you looking sharp today?"

Why do bakers put candles on top of birthday cakes?

We wouldn't be able to light them if they were placed underneath the cake.

Why did the boy hit his birthday cake with a hammer?

It was pound cake.

How do you express birthday wishes to a female sheep?

"Happy birthday to ewe."

Birthdays

How long does it take a candle to burn down?

About a wick.

Why were there balloons on the toilet?

It was a birthday potty.

What did one birthday cake candle say to the other?

"Don't birthdays really burn you up?"

What did dad say when he got an alarm clock as a birthday gift?

"There's no time like the present."

Why do people write on birthday cakes?

So you can have your cake and read it too.

Why did the golfer refuse to cut the birthday cake?

He was afraid he would slice it.

Why was the dragon mad on his birthday?

He couldn't blow out his candles.

What do you call a female ghost who is celebrating her birthday?

The birthday ghoul.

Why was the birthday cake candle so in love?

Because it had found its match.

What's the worst thing about working at a candle factory?

You will probably have to work on wick ends.

Why type of birthday parties includes candles on a cake?

A blow-out event.

Who did the buck and doe invite to their fawn's birthday party?

Her deerest friends.

Birthdays

Try These Tongue Twisters

At Bertha's birthday bash, Bob bobbed for bobbled bottle caps.

Kari can cut Ken's cake come cake-cutting time.

"Ice cream," I scream, "Ice cream."

Knock-Knock.

Who's there?
Bertha Day.

Bertha who?
Bertha Day is a reason for us to celebrate having you as a friend.

Knock-Knock.

Who's there?
Osborne.

Osborne who?
Osborne on my birthday.

Knock-Knock.

Who's there?
Abby.

Abby who?
Abby birthday.

Knock-Knock.

Who's there?
Aye, Matey.

Aye, Matey who?
Aye, Matey years old; just kidding, I'm _____. *(Fill in the blank with your age.)*

Knock-Knock.

Who's there?
Grew Some.

Grew Some who?
Grew Some, scary, and smelly describes most zombies.

Knock-Knock.

Who's there?
Gerald.

Gerald who?
Gerald; that's all I'm going to say – you're old.

Knock-Knock.

Who's there?
Harold.

Harold who?
Harold are you today?

Knock-Knock.

Who's there?
Bird.

Bird who?
Bird day greetings to you.

Knock-Knock.

Who's there?
Soup Prize.

Soup Prize who?
Soup Prize party for you; are you surprised?

Knock-Knock.

Who's there?
Burt Day.

Burt Day who?
Burt Day wishes to you, birthday boy.

Knock-Knock.

Who's there?
Pizza.

Pizza who?
Pizza cake, please.

Chapter Four:
Clothing

We wear clothing such as shirts, jeans, and shoes to keep us warm and to protect our feet. We also wear it to decorate our body – I think I look very handsome in my red button-down shirt. Clothes can also show that we are a part of a team, such as sports uniforms or work uniforms.

Clothes have been around since the dawn of civilization, and clothing jokes have been around for almost as long. Here are some good ones.

Why did the mechanic become a fashion model?

He liked to change attire.

What kind of pants do climbers prefer?

Hiked ones.

What did the right shirt tail say to the left shirt tail?

Do you want to hang out later?

What type of prices does Prince Charming pay for his clothes?

Fair retail (fairy tale).

Who won the competition for the best accessory?

The judges couldn't decide, so they announced it was a tie.

Why was the tailor mad at his wife?

She had pushed all his buttons.

Why did the police officer roll up the crook's pants leg an inch?

The chief asked him to cuff him.

Which month's bees can sew and tie knots?

May bee sew; May bee knot.

Why did the snooty girl refuse to wear more than one glove?

She didn't want to wear second-hand clothing.

Where do electricians buy their clothes?

The outlet.

How does a seamstress get people's attention?

"A hem! A hem!"

What did the tailor say when he was told his services were no longer needed?

"Suit yourself."

What type of earrings do basketball players prefer?

Hoops.

Clothing

Where do shoe salespeople learn their skills?

Boot camp.

Why isn't the history of t-shirts shared in most schools?

T-Shirts go over most students' heads.

How long is a sock from toe to heel?

A foot.

What did the seamstress say when she saw the hole in the sock?

"Darn it!"

Why did the nun freeze her faded uniform so it was stiff before she dyed it black?

Old habits dye hard.

What part of the sock helps people get well?

The heel.

Why did the painter go to the clothing shop?

He needed a second coat.

What kind of hat do snowmen like?

Ice caps.

What kind of button won't unbutton?

A belly button.

What did the tailor say to the sewing machine repairman when he said he could fix his machine?

"Make it sew."

How is a mean king like a boy complaining about his neckwear?

One is a tyrant and the other a tie-rant.

Why couldn't the boy with a broken zipper board the airplane?

He was on the no-fly list.

Why was the pillow-stuffer so sad?

He kept feeling down.

What did the underwear say to the hat?

"You go on ahead; I'll cover the rear."

Clothing

What item does a pig like to wear?

A tie. You've heard of a pig's tie, haven't you?

How do you describe someone who can quickly be talked into wearing leather?

Easily suede.

What kind of cap do drummers like?

A high hat.

What did the railroad engineer wear to the formal banquet?

A railroad tie.

How was the tailor's day going?

Sew-sew.

What jacket should you wear to the first meal of the day?

A breakfast wrap.

Why do people put their trust in the hat-wearing man with the toupee?

He knows how to keep secrets under his hat.

Why was the comedian in the fabric store?

He was looking for material.

What do railroad engineers wear to relax?

Track suits.

What do you call the lie you tell when you say a shirt fits you, but it really doesn't?

A stretch.

What do successful embroidery stores always have?

Initial success.

What size of clothes do psychics wear?

Medium.

What has four wheels and flies?
(Hint: It's not a garbage truck.)

A truck full of zippers.

Why did the boy return his newly purchased shoes to the store?

One of the shoes wasn't right.

Why did the lazy girl join the nudist camp?

She hated doing laundry.

Why did the jalapeno put on a jacket?

It was a little chili.

Why did the man wear a spike-covered vest to the church service?

He wanted to be sharply dressed.

Where are nudists' camps located?

In the middle of no wear.

What kind of clothes are made out of playing cards?

Suits.

Clothing

What's a mom showing when she does laundry without complaining?

Loads of love.

What was the problem with the outfit made of playing cards?

It was hard to fold.

What should you use to tote underwear in public?

A briefcase.

Teacher: Is it easy to find an alternative to the button and zipper?

Student: It's a snap!

If you always keep both of your feet on the ground,
you will never experience the joy of wearing blue jeans –
or any other pants for that matter.

A twenty-year-old girl and her mother were shopping
for clothes one day in a department store.

"What do you think about this one?" her mom asked,
holding up a flowered-print dress.

**"That would make the person who wears it look 40!"
the girl said in frustration.**

Overhearing the conversation, a 60-year-old woman approached them and said
"If that's true and you all aren't going to buy it, can I have it?"

✦ • • • ✦ • • • • • • ✦ • • • ✦

**A customer looked fruitlessly around the store and finally
turned to a clerk and said,
"Don't you have any camouflage pants?
I have looked around this whole store and don't see any."**

The salesclerk replied, "Of course you don't see any.
They wouldn't be good camouflage pants if you saw them."

✦ • • • ✦ • • • • • • ✦ • • • ✦

Try These Tongue Twisters

When the box broke, Bubba's buttons bounced but
Beth's bubble bath bubbles banged, bopped, and burst.

"See, she sees shoes", she says..

Pete's plain pleated pants plainly pleaded Pete,
"Please put Pete's plain pleated pants on."

Clothing

Knock-Knock.

Who's there?
A Boot.

A Boot who?
A Boot time we told some more knock-knock jokes, don't you think?

Knock-Knock.

Who's there?
One Z.

One Z who?
One Z is an item of clothing that babies and toddlers usually wear.

Knock-Knock.

Who's there?
A Shoe.

A Shoe who?
Bless you; that sneeze sounded terrible.

Knock-Knock.

Who's there?
Needle.

Needle who?
Needle the help I can get.

Knock-Knock.

Who's there?
Suit.

Suit who?
**Suit (soot) is what Santa gets on his clothing
as he slides down the chimney.**

Knock-Knock.

Who's there?
Tie.

Tie who?
Tie (Thai) food is similar to Chinese food, but it's a little spicier.

Knock-Knock.

Who's there?
A Dress.

A Dress who?
A Dress each of the invitations, and don't forget the zip code.

Knock-Knock.

Who's there?
Bad Mitten.

Bad Mitten who?
Bad Mitten is a lot like tennis; want to play?

Knock-Knock.

Who's there?
Soft Wear.

Soft Wear who?
Soft Wear are computer programs.

Knock-Knock.

Who's there?
Button.

Button who?
Button into other people's conversations is rude.

Knock-Knock.

Who's there?
Button.

Button who?
Button (but on) my list of things to do, I still have homework.

Knock-Knock.

Who's there?
Button.

Button who?
Button case you are wondering, I knew I was saying "Button" again.

Knock-Knock.

Who's there?
Seamstress.

Seamstress who?
Seamstress about something; can I do anything to reduce the stress?

Knock-Knock.

Who's there?
Night Towel.

Night Towel who?
Night Towel goes, "Who, who?" outside my window.

Knock-Knock.

Who's there?
Jacket.

Jacket who?
Jacket two oranges; I ate two apples.

Chapter Five:
Computers

Can you imagine life without computers? My grandpa lived before the calculator became common, and he said they had to use slide rulers in high school math. Believe it or not, we are among the first generation to grow up with computers and to take them for granted as a part of daily life.

Computers have introduced a whole new set of words into the English language. For instance, grandpa never "Googled". Meanwhile, words that grandpa did know, such as "mouse," "monitor," "text", and "windows" all took on new meanings when computers became common. Computers have also brought about a lot of new jokes. Here are some of my favorites.

Why was the computer drafting and design student so upset with his report card?

It was 3-D.

Why did the software programmer feel hopeless?

On his keyboard he had lost "control" and there was no "escape."

Why did the generous diner make a terrible IT team member?

He kept wanting to tip the servers.

What should you do if you find a good website about how to make sausage?

Send me the link.

Can computers catch head-colds?

I don't know, but I do know they can get bugs.

Why did the IT Department hire Santa Claus?

He had lots of experience with cookies.

What's the difference between a spy and a computer?

A spy has inside intel; a computer has Intel inside.

What is the astronaut's favorite key on the keyboard?

The space bar.

Why did the computer go to the gym?

It wanted to get toner.

What language is used the most in programming?

Foul.

What was unique about the Bluetooth developer's child?

It came out cordless.

Where does a pirate store computer data?

The Arrr drive.

Why was the AI (artificial intelligence) robot financially broke?

It had lost its cache.

Computers

Why did the boy attach his charging cord to the milk carton?

The milk was at 2%.

Why didn't the computer cable want to be Valentine's with the electrical outlet?

There was no connection.

Why did the man kick his computer?

The tech told him to boot it.

Why did the IT professional piloting the airplane put the plane into reverse?

He wanted to back-up into the cloud.

Why did the computer tell a joke?

It saw its mother bored.

Why was the IT technician so angry?

He had a chip on his shoulder.

Why are global position system (GPS) apps so addictive?

People are lost without them.

Why was the seamstress in the chat group?

She was looking for a thread.

How is the Internet like grandma?

Both ask if you will accept cookies.

Why was the computer shy?

It had both software and hardware, but it had no underwear.

Where is haircut data stored on a computer?

The mane frame.

Why was the IT (Information Technology) tech nicknamed "computer"?
(Hint: It's not because he was brainy.)

Left unsupervised for ten minutes, he would go to sleep.

Who were the first computer gurus in North America?

The As Techs.

Why don't you ever see an elephant working at a computer terminal?

Elephants are afraid of mice.

Why did the IT pro call the plumber?

He had a back-up.

Why did the baseball player close his website?

He wasn't getting any hits.

Why don't most Bluetooth devices float?

They are designed to sync.

Why did the spy quit?

He couldn't hack it anymore.

Computers

How do you learn computing skills?

Bit by bit.

What dance is required to make many computers give you access?

The two-step authorization.

What kind of computer program can greet people in any language?

A "hi" tech one.

Where did the supervisor send the delinquent IT professional?

Boot camp.

What was the original pop-up blocker?

The kid who was scared of jack-in-the box.

Who were the first people to fall in love on the net?

Trapeze artists.

Why couldn't the computer fall asleep?

It was too wired.

Why do IT Techs like to sit by computers?

They like to be near Windows.

What kind of computer program can find unsealed ketchup bottles?

Open sauce software.

What kind of dogs do IT professionals prefer?

Computer labs.

Why don't keyboards sleep?

They have two shifts.

What was it like to see the robot's stomach get repaired?

It was gut-wrenching.

What's the advantage of having a fever and a rash?

You have personal hot spots.

How do we get circuit boards?

Are they cut from circuit trees?

Computers

What sound does the clock in the IT Office make?

Tech talk. Tech talk. Tech talk.

What is the most valuable key on the keyboard?

A keyboard without a period (full stop) has no point.

What did the copier have on its toast?

Paper jam.

What kind of coat did the computer tech wear?

Down-loaded.

Why did the IT professional look in the freezer?

He was told the computer screen was frozen.

Why don't IRS computer keyboards have backspace buttons?

The IRS doesn't make mistakes.

What type of horse has trouble keeping apps on its phone?

The app-a-loose-a.

How are programmers and exterminators alike?

They both fight bugs.

What should you do if an ant walks across your keyboard?

Try to get it under "control".

Why was the fitness trainer brought into the IT room?

To work out all the bugs.

What kind of bees make themselves at home in computers in central North America?

U.S. bees.

What did the computer salesman say when someone pointed out a creepy crawly and announced, "I see a bug."

The computer salesman replied, "We don't have bugs; we have features."

The boss got upset when the young administrative assistant tried to use the wrong color of ink.

He looked at her and sternly said, "Don't use that tone with me, missy!"

Computer techs can be nerds.

When I went to the restaurant with one,
I ordered hash-browns; he ordered #browns.

As a student sat in the classroom playing on his phone, the teacher asked rhetorically, "Do you know how much time is wasted on the phone?"

The boy replied, "I don't know, teacher. Let's Google it."

Try These Tongue Twisters

Connie Conner's computer computed quarterly
computer quotas quickly.

Clyde's clean keyboard is in the cupboard
by the cup board.

"Larry and Lisa laid Larry's LAN line last Labor Day,"
Lonnie lied loudly.

Computers

Knock-Knock.

Who's there?
Link In.

Link In who?
Link In was the sixteenth President of the United States.

Knock-Knock.

Who's there?
Ransomware.

Ransomware who?
Ransomware - I don't remember where - but I'm back now.

Knock-Knock.

Who's there?
Iphone.

Iphone who?
I phone my friends when I have a question about homework.

Knock-Knock.

Who's there?
Modem.

Modem who?
Modem weeds down; mowed the grass too.

Chapter Six:
Dentists

I know that dentists are our friends, but that doesn't mean that I like to go visit them at their offices. However, going to the dentist on a regular basis for a check-up is a good habit – and you may get a free toothbrush. I always like to hear that I don't have any cavities, so I brush my teeth regularly.

Your teeth are a major part of your smile. Here are some jokes to smile at.

Why should you always brush your teeth with a friend?

Because most dentists say that brushing alone does not get one's teeth clean.

Why did the dog breeder visit the dentist?

One of his canines was in pain.

What happened when the dentist was too sick to fix a cavity?

He had another dentist fill in.

Dentists

What did the dentist receive for winning Dentist of the Year?

A little plaque.

Why did the dentist appear so sad?

He looked down in the mouth.

Why did the woman start to tell the dentist all her deepest secrets?

The dentist had asked her to open up.

Why did the rude dentist have to make a second mold of the teeth?

He made a terrible first impression.

Why did the jockey go to the dentist?

To get a triple crown.

Why did the male deer go to the dentist to get braces?

He had buck teeth.

Why did the dentist want to do dental work on the girl eating tortillas?

She had a chipped tooth.

Is putting false teeth on a boomerang a good idea?

No; it will likely come back to bite you.

Why did the computer go to the dentist?

To get his byte checked.

What did the dentist suggest on the roller coaster?

"Open up and say 'Ahhhhhhhhhhhhhhh!'"

What is another term for "x-ray" at the dentist's office?

"Tooth pic."

What should you do if you have sensitive teeth?

Don't tease them, don't gossip about them, and don't pull pranks on them.

What did the sailor become when he agreed to take all the pulled teeth from the dentist's office to the other side of the lake?

The tooth ferry.

What did one tooth say to the other tooth on Valentine's Day?

"The dentist is taking me out tonight."

Dentist: You need a crown.

Prince: Finally, someone who understands me.

Dentists

Try These Tongue Twisters

Dennis the dentist dent his dental drill daily drilling dangerous dried decay.

Pearl E. White's pearly whites were pearly, right?

Flo's fluoride flowed right like a flow ride.

Knock-Knock.

Who's there?
Tooth.

Tooth who?
Tooth is, I love telling jokes.

Knock-Knock.

Who's there?
Dennis.

Dennis who?
Dennis is the person who checks your teeth for cavities.

Knock-Knock.

Who's there?
Decayed.

Decayed who?
Decayed is ten years; century is 100.

Knock-Knock.

Who's there?
Denture.

Denture who?
Denture new toy, and your mom will be mad.

Knock-Knock.

Who's there?
Tooth.

Tooth who?
Tooth-in or too fat is not good to be.

Knock-Knock.

Who's there
Hal Itosis.

Hal Itosis who?
Hal Itosis is another word for bad breath.

Knock-Knock.

Who's there?
2:30.

2:30 who?
2:30; can you make it stop hurting?

Knock-Knock.

Who's there?
Filling.

Filling who?
Filling like telling a bunch more knock-knock jokes?

Chapter Seven:
Firefighters

Emergencies can occur at any time, and it is good to know that firefighters, police officers, and other first responders will put their lives on the line for the rest of us. Sometimes some funny things happen on the way to the fire. Here are some smoking hot jokes about firefighters.

At the fire, why do firemen walk around with an axe?

Because it's no drill.

How was the fire at the post office contained?

It was stamped out.

How do you become a fire chief?

Like all jobs, you have to climb the ladder at work.

Who did the firefighter marry?

An old flame.

What professional is usually greeted warmly upon entering a home?

The firefighter.

Why did the firefighter retire?

His career went up in smoke.

Why were so many of the firefighters sick after the clock factory fire?

Too much second-hand smoke.

Why was the boy nervous about making the campfire?

He had burning questions.

Why did the firefighter rescue the calendar from the burning building?

He wanted to save the day.

Why do crows make excellent smoke detectors?

If you have smoke, there is caws for alarm.

Which month reminds campers to put out their fires?

No ember.

What do you say about a stuntman who has successfully jumped from a burning building once again?

"That guy is on fire."

Why was the firefighter so concerned when he saw a magazine on fire in a trashcan?

It was a burning issue.

What did one bonfire coo to the other on Valentine's Day?

"You're hot."

Why did the fire chief insist his people wear uniforms?

He didn't want any casual tees.

Firefighters

Two women are trapped in a burning building.

The first one calls, "Help! Help!" to the firefighters below.

The firefighters appear not to hear her, so the other woman calls,
"Up here! We need help!"

The firefighters still apparently cannot hear or see them;
therefore, one woman suggests, "Let's yell together."

The second one nods in agreement.
"Together! Together! Together!"

An American July 4 tradition begins:

Caveman: Grog invent fire. Let's celebrate. Fire works!

Try These Tongue Twisters

Five fire flames fired flames feverishly.

Ashe asked if fresh ash acts as fast as ashy ash acts.

Jose hooked Hose A to the high hydrant.

Knock-Knock.

Who's there?
Jose.

Jose who?
Jose goes on the first fire hydrant;
Hose B goes on the second.

Knock-Knock.

Who's there?
Bernie.

Bernie who?
Bernie campfire but be careful
not to start a wildfire.

Knock-Knock.

Who's there?
Ash.

Ash who?
Bless you.

Knock-Knock.

Who's there?
Reece Ponder.

Reece Ponder who?
Reece Ponders are people like ambulance drivers, firefighters, and police officers.

Knock-Knock.

Who's there?
Bert.

Bert who?
Bert the toast and set off the smoke alarm.

Knock-Knock.

Who's there?
Our Son.

Our Son who?
Our Son (arson) means setting first to something that is not yours.

Knock-Knock.

Who's there?
Fall Tea.

Fall Tea who?
Fall Tea wiring can lead to house fires.

Knock-Knock.

Who's there?
M. Burr.

M. Burr who?
M. Burr of the campfire may still be hot; be careful.

Knock-Knock.

Who's there?
Friar Tuck.

Friar Tuck who?
Friar Tuck is the vehicle that takes firefighters to the fire.

Knock-Knock.

Who's there?
Ample Fire.

Ample Fire who?
Ample Fire (amplifier) makes most stereo systems sound better.

Chapter Eight:
Food

One thing that every human being has in common is the need to eat. Another thing in common is the desire to laugh. Here are some jokes that combine the two – jokes about food. You'll eat them up!

Which type of meat predicts the future and tells fortunes?

Medium steak.

How is a gold miner like a chef?

They both judge success by what's in the pan.

Why did the barista at the coffee shop gossip?

She had no filter.

Who keeps everyone calm
in the kitchen?

The peas maker.

Did the baker think it would be easy
to make something out of an egg,
flour, and sugar?

Yes. He said it would be a piece of cake.

Did you hear about the man who made
fried vegetables in his sleep?

He was sleep wokking.

What was the cowboy's status when
he got buttermilk dressing
on his fingers and palms?

Ranch hand.

What spice do cooks in prison rely on?

If they are in prison, they are
serving thyme.

Is cooking dangerous?

It can be whisky.

Why was the grocery cart sad?

It was tired of getting pushed around.

Why did the umpire decline a chair
at the restaurant?

He liked to stand behind the plate.

Why did the softball team recruit
the baker?

The team needed a new batter.

Why can't you trust
a deli sandwich?

They are full of bologna.

What did the grocery store stocker say
when he was given the box of sausages?

"This is the wurst case."

How do you crack up a walnut?

You tell it a nutty joke.

Food

What is the worst tasting tea?

Nas Tea.

Which roll does a pastry chef like best?

The payroll.

Why should you not get too attached to tea?

Tea leaves.

What part of a bread loaf is snooty?

The upper crust.

Which food is the laziest?

The bread loafs.

What's a glutton's favorite number?

Ate.

Why is the knife the king of the silverware?

The others just don't cut it.

What did salt say to pepper?

"What's shaking?"

What would happen if margarine and spreads no longer existed?

The world would be a butter place.

What should you wear to a tea party?

A t-shirt.

How does spaghetti come up with ideas?

It uses the ol' noodle.

What's the best way to sell Life Savers candy?

In mint condition.

Why did the ice-cream truck break down?

Because of the rocky road.

What happened when the Earl Grey lover was accidently given coffee?

It wasn't his cup of tea.

Food

Which is more useful; a spoon or a fork?

The fork; the spoon is pointless.

Why was the butter so unhappy with the movie director?

It didn't like the rolls it was being assigned.

Is it okay to make a mistake making a pie?

Of course; everyone knows it's not a piece of cake.

Was the candy man rich?

Yes. He made a mint.

How is going to the doughnut shop like going to the golf course?

There's a chance of seeing a hole in one.

What does every trainee at the doughnut shop receive?

A list of dos and doughnuts.

Did you read the chef's autobiography?

It has a lot of stirring parts.

Try These Tongue Twisters

Friar Fred fixed the fried food fryer.

Gary's garlic-grilled grains gave Gus great weight gains.

Bet he bought Betty bits of buttered broccoli bites.

Knock-Knock.

Who's there?
Brownies.

Brownies who?
Brownies, green C's, red D's, and blue F's add a lot of color to the bulletin-board.

Knock-Knock.

Who's there?
In Pudding.

In Pudding who?
In Pudding data into a computer takes time.

Knock-Knock.

Who's there?
Fried Egg.

Fried Egg who?
Fried Egg is my favorite day of the week.

Knock-Knock.

Who's there?
Olive.

Olive who?
Olive my jokes are funny, aren't they?

Food

Knock-Knock.

Who's there?
Turnover.

Turnover who?
Turnover your test once everyone has their copy.

Knock-Knock.

Who's there?
Kikkoman.

Kikkoman who?
Kikkoman when he's down, and you may get disqualified from your boxing match.

Knock-Knock.

Who's there?
Bagel.

Bagel who?
Bagels fly over the bay; seagulls fly over the sea.

Knock-Knock.

Who's there?
Candy Man.

Candy Man who?
Candy Man get the car repaired for us?

Knock-Knock.

Who's there?
Cokes.

Cokes who?
Cokes (coax) the cat to come out from under the chair; it's scared of us.

Knock-Knock.

Who's there?
Fondue.

Fondue who?
Fondue to be born any day, mom and dad deer will be great parents.

Knock-Knock.

Who's there?
Meat Tin.

Meat Tin who?
Meat Tin after school for a game of football; can you come?

Knock-Knock.

Who's there?
Mayo.

Mayo who?
Mayo may not be another joke after this.

Chapter Nine:
Gardens

I don't know about you, but I love planting something and watching it grow throughout the summer. It is hard to believe that one tiny seed can become a giant corn stalk with so many kernels I can't count them all.

(Fun fact: Did you know that the average ear of corn has sixteen rows?)

In addition to seeds, I also like to plant smiles. Here are some gardening jokes that will likely grow a smile on your face.

Why don't trees have teeth?

They are all bark and no bite.

Gardens

How did the police describe the stolen yam?

They said it was a hot potato.

**Why did the corn plant
go to the doctor?**

It had an earache.

**How did the gardener show his
vegetables to his friends?**

Tastefully.

**What do you do with
a self-centered potato?**

Butter it up.

**What's the most popular language
in the garden?** *(Hint: It's not English.)*

Spinach.

**How did the comedian poke fun
at the garden?**

He roasted the vegetables.

**What root-vegetables is long,
cream-colored, and whispers
in the garden?**

The hoarse radish.

What plants are electrical?

Power plants.

Why is it difficult to win an argument against a cactus?

They have a lot of good points.

Why was Momma Cucumber worried about her son?

She thought he was in a pickle.

Why was there an anti-bullying seminar held in the garden?

The wheelbarrow was always getting pushed around.

Why do most gardeners recall their first shovel-full of dirt?

It was a ground-breaking moment.

What kind of spies are found in many gardens?

Moles.

Why did the unsuccessful gardener join a band?

He had lots of sick beets to offer.

What kind of spyware is found in most gardens?

Bugs.

What kind of glasses should you wear so you don't strain your eyes looking for unwanted plants in your garden?

Your weeding glasses.

What was the nervous, talkative gardener's assistant told when he blabbered about what to do with the leftover watermelon?

"Can it."

Gardens

Which garden vegetable has the most jewelry?

The onion; it has a lot of rings.

How is a garden like the ocean?

Both give you a "see food" experience.

What did the auto mechanic expect to grow in his garden?

A bumper crop.

Why did the novelist add topsoil to his garden?

He always liked it when a plot thickened.

Which vegetables prefer to work in groups?

Lettuce and cabbage; they believe two heads are better than one.

To have a great garden, what kind of water drops must hit the soil?

Perspiration.

What did the two seeds say as they began the race to sprout out of the soil?

"Ready, set, grow!"

Which flower never forgets to send its dad a Father's Day card?

The son flower.

What flower is known for sleeping during the day?

The day-z-z-z-z-z-z-z-z-z.

What did the baker try to grow in his garden?

Flours.

What kind of dog can find corn?

A corn dog.

Which fruit is the most charismatic?

A strawberry smoothie.

What do you call the wisdom found in a book on how to grow herbs?

Sage advice.

Is it okay to put a peach in the freezer?

Doesn't the U.S. constitution say something about us having the right to freeze peach?

Should grapes be measured in metrics or in the U.S. customary system?

The U.S. system; after all, this are vine "yards", not vine "meters".

Do artists who paint pictures of a garden work for hourly wages?

No; most draw a celery.

What are you doing if you inform people that grapes will dry out and become raisins?

Raisin awareness.

Gardens

Why did the gardener keep away from the watermelon?

The watermelon was a seedy character.

What did the gardener conclude when he struck rocky soil?

It wasn't going to be a bed of roses.

Which vegetable is the nicest?

The sweet potato.

How did the two strawberries greet each other?

With a strawberry shake.

Why did the chicken farmer decide to grow a garden as well as raise chickens?

He thought outside the bawks.

How successful was the gardener who tried to grow just vegetables?

His efforts were fruitless.

Why were the plants so proud to be a part of the garden?

They had deep roots.

Which vegetable succumbs
to flattery?

The potatoes like to be buttered up.

How is an ordinary potato like a sports
announcer?

Both are common 'tators.

How can you repair
a broken tomato?

With tomato paste.

Which vegetable is sometimes
ridiculously silly?

Broccoli is often cheesy.

Which vegetable is the kindest?

Lettuce; lettuce has a heart.

Which vegetable persists
through adversity?

The beet goes on.

Try These Tongue Twisters

Gary grew some gruesome gray-green gourds.

Garden guard Garth guardedly guarded gaudy gardens.

Bea's beaten beet's butter better beat Bea's beaten beet to the buffet board.

Gardens

Knock-Knock.

Who's there?
Thyme

Thyme who?
Thyme to tell some knock-knock jokes.

Knock-Knock.

Who's there?
Pickle.

Pickle who?
Pickle little flower to put in the vase, please.

Knock-Knock.

Who's there?
Daisies.

Daisies who?
Daisies very active; other days he's very tired.

Knock-Knock.

Who's there?
Bean.

Bean who?
Bean there; done that.

Knock-Knock.

Who's there?
Lilac.

Lilac who?
Lilac that and you'll be a great politician or a used car salesperson.

Knock-Knock.

Who's there?
Reseeding.

Reseeding who?
Reseeding hairlines aren't fun; dad will be bald in a few more years.

Knock-Knock.

Who's there?
Thistle.

Thistle who?
Thistle be a lot of fun.

Knock-Knock.

Who's there?
Garden.

Garden who?
Garden (guarding) the vegetables so the rabbits won't eat them.

Knock-Knock.

Who's there?
Trowel.

Trowel who?
Trowels and tribulations are a part of gardening.

Knock-Knock.

Who's there?
A Rose.

A Rose who?
A Rose out of bed this morning, ready to face the day.

Knock-Knock.

Who's there?
Eaton Wright.

Eaton Wright who?
Eaton Wright out of the garden, and that food is delicious.

Knock-Knock.

Who's there?
Peas.

Peas who?
Peas keep telling more knock-knock jokes.

Knock-Knock.

Who's there?
Cherry.

Cherry who?
Cherry people are much more fun to be around than sad people.

Chapter Ten:
Haircuts

Getting one's haircut can be a very stressful time. Your barber may be your mom or it may be a professional. One never knows what one will look like after a haircut. Haircuts, though, are a part of life, and therefore they are a part of this joke book.

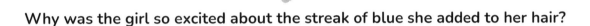

Why was the girl so excited about the streak of blue she added to her hair?

It was a personal highlight.

Why does the barber keep scissors?

For shear fun.

What happened when the comedian told the hairdresser a joke?

The hairdresser dyed laughing.

What type of music groups does hair like to listen to?

Hair bands.

Why do barbers gossip so much?

They enjoy talking behind other people's backs.

Why did the newscaster become a barber?

He loved showing highlights.

Is a man's wig for $1 a good deal?

It's a small price toupee.

Why did the long-haired girl take an extra hotdog role?

She wanted to wear her hair in a bun.

What's a haircut smell like?

A breath of fresh hair.

Why was the barber considered to be a bully?

He teased hair.

Haircuts

What exercise do barbers do?

Curls.

What do you call the reduced or sale price of haircuts?

The cut rate.

Why did the birdwatcher's wife bring the barber to her husband?

Her husband refused to go indoors until he had seen "one mo' hawk".

What kind of gun does the barber prefer?

One with a hair trigger.

If your dad's balding hairline looks like the flap of an envelope, what does he have?

Mail pattern baldness.

How do bees wear their hair?

In buzz cuts.

What's similar between a barber and a pet shop owner at Easter?

Both are into hare management.

What did the barber do in his new role on the arson investigation team?

He combed through the ashes.

How are hair shavings on the floor similar to factory smoke?

One is hair pollution, and the other is air pollution.

How is a flattop haircut similar to a pirate laying off a first mate?

One is a crewcut, and the other is a crew cut.

How significant is the career decision of choosing between being the one who cuts hair and the one who colors hair?

It's do or die.

How do people describe a rude barber?

"He's a bit snippy."

How is a line of people waiting for a haircut similar to people attending a cookout?

One is a barber queue, and the other is a barbeque.

Was the barber gutsy to put a dish upside-down on top of the customer's head and then trim his hair?

It was a bowled move.

What did the geometry teacher like best about combing hair?

The wrecked tangles.

How did the spy describe his toupee?

"It's top secret."

Haircuts

Why is summer bald men's favorite season?

It's their chance to shine.

What hairstyle did the kid with fireworks prefer?

Bangs.

Was the loose hair impressed with the hairdryer?

It was blown away

How did the Hollywood actor want his hair styled?

He wanted a big part.

Which of the barber's tools tells tall tales?

The hair dryer is full of hot air.

Why did the barber bring the tree hair dye?

Because he could see its roots.

What's the difference between an ordinary piece of hair and a Boeing 747?

One is a hair plain and the other is an airplane.

Where do sheep go to get their hair cut?

The baa-baa shop.

What type of rabbit do men stick on their chins?

Facial hares.

Why do barbers charge for a good brushing to remove tangles?

Because it's knot free.

What prize did the beautician win in high school?

Home combing queen.

How is a friend inviting you over similar to a man taking long hair from the side of his head and placing it over the top of his bald spot?

One is "come over here" and the other is "comb over hair".

Why did the barber hesitate to comb the tangles out of the policewoman's hair?

He had never had a brush with the law.

What makes a great parting gift?

A comb.

Why did the bagel store owner go to the barber?

He wanted to get his locks trimmed.

What was so great about the documentary about barbers?

It had lots of clips.

What animal helps to hold one's hair in place?

Moose.

Haircuts

What did the man with no hair and the crying baby have in common?

Both bawled.

Is going to the barber shop to get a haircut scary?

It's a hair-razing experience.

How is a haircut like a sale?

It is 90% off.

What did Momma Wig say to Junior Wig?

"I'll teach you how to get a head in life."

How can you tell that barbering is a respected profession?

Men take their hats off in the presence of a barber.

Why did the barber say that he had retired?

He just couldn't cut it anymore.

Why did the Christmas tree go to the barber?

It needed trimming.

Why did the barber place his scissors and clippers in the refrigerator?

He wanted to give cool haircuts.

Why was the hair no longer friends with the bald man's head?

I don't know, but they fell out.

Customer: Waiter, there's a hair in my soup.

Waiter: Were you expecting a whole toupee?

A customer walks into a barber shop and states, "I'd like a comb, please."

The barber asks, "Steel?"

The man replies, "No, I'll pay."

A little boy was in need of a haircut.
His dad offered, "I'll cut it for you."

**As the boy climbed hesitantly onto a kitchen chair, he asked,
"Do you have any experience?"**

"I've done it a number of times," his dad replied, clippers in hand.

**After receiving the haircut the boy looked in the mirror –
and was horrified. He ran to his dad sobbing,
"I thought you said you had given haircuts a number of times."**

"Zero is a number," his dad affirmed.

Haircuts

Try These Tongue Twisters

Barber Bob botched Bobbi's bob.

Kevin carefully kept Cliff's crewcut cut close

Connie's Cut and Curl cut and curled curly curls.

Knock-Knock.

Who's there?
Combing.

Combing who?
Combing up with lots more good jokes.

Knock-Knock.

Who's there?
Mustache.

Mustache who?
Mustache you, are you having a good time?

Knock-Knock.

Who's there?
Chester.

Chester who?
Chester and back hair are two things many barbers don't trim for most customers.

Knock-Knock.

Who's there?
Barber Q.

Barber Q. who?
Barber Q. at my place; you bring the meat and I'll cook it on the grill.

Knock-Knock.

Who's there?
Razor.

Razor who?
Razor hand if you know the answer.

Knock-Knock.

Who's there?
Barb Burr.

Barb Burr who?
Barb Burr will trim your hair for you.

Knock-Knock.

Who's there?
Bald.

Bald who?
Bald my eyes out when I saw how bad my last haircut was.

Knock-Knock.

Who's there?
Hairy.

Hairy who?
Hairy up or we're going to miss the bus.

Knock-Knock.

Who's there?
Toupee.

Toupee who?
Toupee for something is to buy it; to not pay is to steal it.

Knock-Knock.

Who's there?
Hair.

Hair who?
Hair I am, knocking on your door.

84

Chapter Eleven:
Health

I've heard that an apple a day will keep the doctor away. That may be true; I have never had a doctor come to see me at my house. However, I have gone to the doctor several times. I've been to get seen when I've been sick, and I've gone to get vaccines when I am well.

I've also heard that laughter is the best medicine. Perhaps laughter about doctors is the best medicine of all. I hope it is. Here is a healthy dose of doctor humor.

What did the doctor with the big ego ask his patient to say?

"Say 'Ah . . . some!'"

What did the doctor say to the anxious man who was shrinking?

"You're going to have to be a little patient."

Why did the shoes go to the doctor?

They needed to be healed.

An apple a day may keep the doctor away, but what can you eat to keep the teacher away?

An onion.

Why wasn't the optimist upset when he could not turn his neck?

He knew he had a lot he could still look forward to.

Why did the doctor believe the TV was paranoid?

The TV said someone was always watching it.

Why did the Teddy Bear go to the doctor?

Its nose was stuffy.

What happened after the boy drank the formula that made him invisible?

He had to go to the E.R. (emergency room) to be seen.

Have you ever tried acupuncture, that therapy where the doctors stick pins into you?

It may or may not work, but it definitely has some points.

What body parts are the most reliable?

You can always count on your fingers and toes.

What did the doctor say when the salad told him it was feeling bland?

"That's a problem that needs addressing (a dressing)."

Why did the leaf have to go to the hospital?

It had a bad fall.

What is the first step of overcoming the fear of eating at all-you can-eat buffets?

You have to be willing to help yourself.

Health

Why did the basketball star's feet itch?

He had athlete's foot.

When the man brought his vacuum to the doctor's receptionist, what did he tell her?

"I need to get my vac seen."

Was the doctor confident that he could remove the tick?

Yes. He believed he could pull it off.

What did the doctor determine was wrong with the car?

It had a lot of gas.

What did the doctor caution when showing children his pet bee?

"This might sting a little."

What did the boy allergic to bees worry he was going to break out in?

Hives.

Why did the accountant go to the doctor?

He wasn't feeling two grand.

Why did the ham go to the doctor?

It wanted to be cured.

Why did the pillow go to the doctor?

It felt stuffed up.

Which doctor has the biggest ego?

The I doctor.

What happened after the heart patient decided against getting a heart transplant?

He later had a change of heart.

Why did the cheapskate duck want to see the plastic surgeon?

She wanted to get her bill reduced.

What's the problem with having migraines?

They're a real headache.

Why did the oyster visit the doctor?

He pulled a mussel.

What was the gingerbread man doing after he hurt his leg?

Icing it.

Why did the hypochondriac go to the doctor?

Because he had the uncommon cold.

What did the doctor advise the nervous nurse?

"Just give your best shot."

Why did the farmer have to go to the doctor after walking his pet pig on a leash?

He had pulled his ham string.

Health

Why was the duck banned from the doctor's office?

Because it kept yelling, "Quack," for all the patients to hear.

Why did the doctor advise the clown to remove his red nose before going to bed?

He didn't want him to sleep funny.

Why don't they have quiz games at the hospital to cheer up the patients?

Because the irritable doctor said, "Don't test my patience."

The doctor approached a patient who was lying in the hospital bed and asked him, "How are you feeling today?"

The man replied, "Mostly with my fingers."

Patient: I threw my back out.

Doctor: Show me which dumpster, and I'll help you look for it.

What happened when the doctor told the math teacher he needed to start an IV?

The math teacher replied, "I love Roman numerals."

Dr. Apple: Have I told you about the new germ I found?

Dr. Banana: No. Tell me.

Dr. Apple: On second thought, I shouldn't spread it.

Eye Doctor: I want you to put your hand over your good eye and then tell me what you see.

Patient: A palm.

I tried my best, but I only got one question right on the human anatomy test.

At least my heart was in the right place.

Have you tried the Summer Diet?

On that diet, you can have summer this and summer that . . .

Health

Try These Tongue Twisters

Doctor Danielle doctored Dan's rough dandruff during Dan's rough development of dandruff.

Sure, Shirely, surely shots are sure shots.

Pete's panic peaked when Pete peeked at the needle prick poking Pete's pal Paul.

Knock-Knock.

Who's there?
Phlegm.

Phlegm who?
Phlegm-ingos are pink birds that often stand on just one foot.

Knock-Knock.

Who's there?
Kleenex.

Kleenex who?
Kleenex (clinics) are a combination emergency room and doctor's office.

Knock-Knock.

Who's there?
Weak back.

Weak back who?
Weak back – or maybe it was two weeks ago – I saw you at school.

Knock-Knock.

Who's there?
A pill.

A pill who?
A pill is tiring; downhill is easy.

Knock-Knock.

Who's there?
Vaccine.

Vaccine who?
Vaccine in the hallway; broom seen by the stairs – you've been cleaning, haven't you?

Knock-Knock.

Who's there?
Surgeon.

Surgeon who?
Surgeon for good jokes; do you know any?

Knock-Knock.

Who's there?
Weak Cough.

Weak Cough who?
Weak Cough (week off) at school coming up for winter break.

Knock-Knock.

Who's there?
Disney.

Disney who?
Disney hurts; this knee doesn't.

Knock-Knock.

Who's there?
Kid Niece.

Kid Niece who?
Kid Niece (kidney's) filter the body's blood supply.

Knock-Knock.

Who's there?
Aiken

Aiken who?
Aiken (aching) people often blame their aches on the weather.

Knock-Knock.

Who's there?
Estella Hertz.

Estella Hertz who?
Estella Hertz; can you make it stop hurting?

Knock-Knock.

Who's there?
Yul B. Alwright.

Yul B. Alwright who?
Yul B. Alwright; the doctor says it's just a nasty cold.

Chapter Twelve:

Knights, Kings, and Queens

Have you ever pretended to be royalty? Most of us have. Who doesn't want to be pampered like a princess or as powerful as a prince?

The Middle Ages may have been long ago, but most of us still revere knights and their heroic quests. It's no wonder then, that jokes about kings and queens are so interesting to us. Here are some good ones; they are so good, in fact, I would declare them fit for a king.

Why did the king's son hire a police detective to replace his maid?

To dust for prince.

What do you call the candles medieval warriors keep on until morning?

Knight lights.

What should you say when tucking a knight into bed?

"Nighty, knight."

How long does a jousting tournament last?

Until knightfall.

What's the difference between Hanukkah and a dragon?

Hanukkah is for eight nights; the dragon ate knights.

Why did the king like to hear his personal weather forecaster predict that falling ice was likely?

He loved to hear the weather forecaster say, "Hail, king."

What did the Middle Age warrior call his pajamas?

His knight gown.

Why did the prince toss his chair across the room?

Because he wanted to sit on a thrown.

What did the king like about playing chess in the evening?

He liked being able to take the knight off.

What did the two men in armor request at the inn?

A room for two knights.

What did people call the friendly king?

Mr. "Hi" and Mighty.

Who is the king of school supplies?

The ruler.

What kind of bird wears armor?

The Knight Owl.

Knights, Kings, and Queens

What was the king's favorite piece of clothing?

His reign jacket.

What does the knight use to see in the dark?

Knight Vision goggles.

What did the knight ask the king at the auction?

"What's your bidding, sire?"

Where did the soldiers of the Middle Ages learn to fight dragons?

Knight School.

Why did the king go to the dentist?

To get a new crown.

What shift does the man in armor have?

The knight shift.

Why was the king's coronation the highlight of his life?

It was his crowning achievement.

What do you call a female horse in armor?

A Knight Mare.

What did the jester pun as the king walked up the hill?

"Hi, king."

Which English king wrote the most books?

King Author.

Try These Tongue Twisters

Jolly John just joined the jovial jousters gesturing at Jack's jazzy jutting jagged jacket.

The parking for the par king was par.

Before going nighty-night, nightly naughty Knight Sir Cull circled the circle circling Circle Square.

Knights, Kings, and Queens

Knock-Knock.

Who's there?
King Dumb.

King Dumb who?
King Dumb is what kings and queens rule over.

Knock-Knock.

Who's there?
You, knighted.

You, knighted who?
You, knighted we stand; divided we fall.

Knock-Knock.

Who's there?
Czar E.

Czar E. who?
Czar E. if one of my jokes offends you.

Knock-Knock.

Who's there?
Maiden.

Maiden who?
Maiden the United States of America.

Knock-Knock.

Who's there?
A King.

A King who?
A King (aching) is all I have done since I ran laps yesterday.

Knock-Knock.

Who's there?
Earl.

Earl who?
Earl-ier you told some great jokes; let's do more!

Knock-Knock.

Who's there?
Throne.

Throne who?
Throne the baseball is a lot of fun.

Knock-Knock.

Who's there?
Dan Saul, Knight.

Dan Saul, Knight who?
Dan Saul, Knight; dance all day too.

Knock-Knock.

Who's there?
Jester.

Jester who?
Jester your friendly little ol' knock-knock buddy.

Knock-Knock.

Who's there?
Serf.

Serf who?
Serf-ing the Internet is fun.

Knock-Knock.

Who's there?
Serf Faces.

Serf Faces.
Serf Faces (surfaces) can be grainy, velvety, smooth, or rough.

Knock-Knock.

Who's there?
Moats.

Moats who?
Moats people enjoy a good knock-knock joke.

Knock-Knock.

Who's there?
Empress.

Empress who?
Empress me with your talent; let's see what you can do.

Knock-Knock.

Who's there?
Sultan.

Sultan who?
Sultan pepper go well with almost every meal.

Chapter Thirteen:
Math & Science

Every day at school we have a time for math and a time for science; I just can't get away from them. Therefore, it is only fitting that there be time in this book for them.

Math has always been a bit confusing to me. I quickly learned that two plus two was four. However, the next day the teacher said that three plus one was four. I remember thinking, yesterday you said two plus two was four; now you've changed it. The next day, she said that one plus three was also four. I got to thinking that everything was four. She said that was not true. Math and science have kept me under stress ever since then – but I refuse to let it beat me.

You've heard of people who laugh at danger? Well, I laugh at math. Here are some of my favorite math and science jokes.

Why did Zero start dating?

He wanted to find the one.

Who tattled on the scientist?

The lab rat.

When asked to come up with a word that starts with the letter "N", what do most people say?

Nothing.

Why shouldn't you judge a calculator by its looks?

Because it is what is inside that counts.

Was the researcher dropping a bowling ball from the roof of a 42-story building an important experiment?

It was a ground-breaking experiment.

Why does the toddler who doesn't know his numbers feel left out?

People told him he doesn't count.

What geometric shape is the smartest?

The circle; it is well-rounded and has 360 degrees.

Why are geometry teachers so logical?

They make good points.

Why is subtraction so hard for many students to understand?

Because in subtraction things don't add up.

What fraction of people is too tense?

One fifth.
(2/10ths - too tense - reduces to 1/5.)

Why did the biologist take the bacteria to the opera?

It was cultured.

What animal makes the most phone calls?

The cell; the cell phones.

Why should you never doubt a 90-degree triangle?

It is always right.

Math & Science

What's so important about abacus beads?

It's the little things that count.

Why did the science teacher begin the year talking about ammonia?

Because it was basic material.

What happened when the vowels appeared before the judge in court?

They were sentenced.

How is nostalgia like a grammar assignment?

We find the past perfect and the present tense.

Which numerals won't sit still?

Roamin' numerals.

What do anthropologists and microbiologists have in common?

Both study a variety of cultures.

Which animal speaks Greek?

The cat says, "Mew".
(Greek for the letter M)

Why did the nerd not give a speech containing all the decimals of pi?

Because he could have gone on forever.

Which is the most respected scientific element?

People speak highly of helium.

Which scientific element is responsible for laughter?

Helium; put two helium molecules together and its "HeHe".

Why did the track runner bring his math book to the starting line of the race with him?

He wanted to run away from his problems.

Why did the obtuse angle go to the beach?

It was over 90 degrees.

What happened when the calculator became unreliable?

You couldn't count on it.

What is a math teacher's favorite fruit?

Ordered pears.

Which school subject is least racist?

Math; math promotes equality.

What did the decimal say to the seemingly-confused number?

"Do you get my point?"

What number talks the most?

pi goes on forever.

What is so great about math?

The addition sign is a big plus.

Why are math teachers great problem solvers?

They always have an angle.

Math & Science

At what temperature do cars run?

Vroom temperature.

What do a microbiologist and a prisoner have in common?

Both study cell walls.

What did Mom say to Junior when she woke him to do his math homework?

"Up and add 'em."

What's the math teacher's favorite Thanksgiving dessert?

Pumpkin pi.

Which is braver, a pebble or a big rock?

The big rock is a little boulder.

Does the helium museum get great reviews?

Most people speak very highly having been there.

What's the difference between a generous genie and a research scientist?

One grants four wishes and the other wishes for grants.

What's the secret to making a good circle?

Take your time; don't cut corners.

What prevented the girl from acing her math quiz covering decimals?

One point.

Why do some people agree with everything other people say?

They don't no.

What is the smartest geometric shape?

The cylinder. The cylinder has graduated and now speaks volumes.

Why was the yardstick single?

He tried to find the right girl, but he never did meter.

Did you hear the joke about the unstamped letter?

Never mind; you won't get it.

What happens if you lose your thesaurus?

The event is so traumatic that you likely won't have the words to describe it.

Math & Science

What is the best way to measure a lawn?

With a yardstick.

What happened when the boy began to enthusiastically read the dictionary word for word?

Within a few days, he was past caring.

What were the first words of the nerdy baby?

"Google dada."

Why should you never debate during an earthquake?

You're on shaky ground.

"I don't like bees and wasps,"
the camper stated as he hiked through the woods with the nature guide.

The nature guide turned around and asked, "What's wrong with bees?"

The boy replied, "I don't know. I just don't like them.
I am okay with every other letter of the alphabet, however."

Two nerds were talking about their biology class.

One said, "For the dissecting unit, the teacher gave me a B."

The other replied, "You're lucky. She gave me a frog."

Some older kids were telling me that the alphabet stopped at the letter T.

Well, guess what?

I am onto you!

Here are some punny traits about shapes:

Circles are well rounded. Squares are all right.
Triangles always have three good points.

Try These Tongue Twisters

"Texas test-tubes test tubes," Tex texted testily.

The seven scientists studying the science of sight sighed silently
and then cited the sight sites scientifically.

Fearlessly Frank figured fractions of factions.

Knock-Knock.

Who's there?
Lois D.

Lois D who?
Lois D. Nominator is what all the fractions you are working with at the time have in common.

Knock-Knock.

Who's there?
Adam.

Adam who?
Adam again; I got a different total than you did.

Knock-Knock.

Who's there?
Auntie Biotic.

Auntie Biotic who?
Auntie Biotics help us to get well when we are sick.

Knock-Knock.

Who's there?
Sum Adder.

Sum Adder who?
Sum Adder with you? you don't seem yourself.

Math & Science

Knock-Knock.

Who's there?
Ed Vance.

Ed Vance who?
Ed Vance math is much harder than basic math.

Knock-Knock.

Who's there?
Cell Laboratory.

Cell Laboratory who?
Cell Laboratory feelings have come over me; let's celebrate; I'm having a great time.

Knock-Knock.

Who's there?
Cy Ince.

Cy Ince who?
Cy Ince is one of my favorite school subjects.

Knock-Knock.

Who's there?
Acid.

Acid who?
Acid hello to you, and you don't reply.

Chapter Fourteen:
Music

Do you like to sing?

I like to sing. I'm not very good at it, but I still like to do it. I sometimes sing in the shower; I'm so good the dog starts howling along. I sing popular songs and I sing songs I make up; no two shower sessions are the same.

Not only do I think up songs in the shower, I think up jokes as well. Here are some noteworthy – did you catch the pun? - jokes about music.

Why was the trumpet player considered a bragger?

He tooted his own horn.

Why did the locksmith become a musician?

He wanted to do something with key changes.

How do you answer a multiple-choice question that you are stuck on in Music History class?

You skip the question and then circle Bach.

What are the rules of music called?

Do-re-mi-fa-so law.

Do you know why I have mixed feelings about elevator music?

Half of the time it is uplifting, but it's a real downer the other half.

What animal plays the triangle?

The bat. You've heard of the dingbat, haven't you?

Music

What is the most musical part of the body?

The nose; you can pick it and you can blow it.

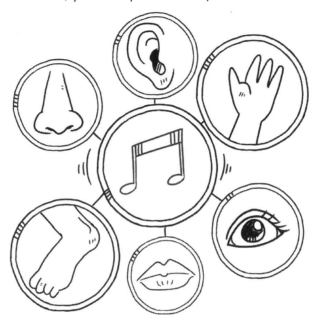

What happened when the student conductor got in trouble and had to lead the orchestra again in practice?

He had to face the music.

What kind of background music should you have to burst balloons?

Pop music.

What happens if you try to make a deal for a guitar in a pawn shop?

It will probably come with strings attached.

What do you call hip hop sheet music?

Rapping paper.

How can you tell that someone is going to be a singing superstar?

Because if they go "do-re-mi" you know they are likely to go fa.

What musical chord do fish prefer?

Fish love scales in general, but they are especially fond of the sea

What musical instrument did the billiards player play?

A cue stick guitar.

What is a surfer's favorite type of music?

New wave.

Why did the electrician become a musician?

He was fascinated with cords.

What kind of music should you play for a psychologist?

A shrink rap.

How do musicians stay in contact with each other?

They touch bass.

What's the difference between a conductor and a criminal?

The criminal doesn't want to face the music.

What timepiece loves music?

The watch; it is usually found in a band.

Music

Why did the drummer have a drum set tattooed on his arm?

He found it very cymbolic.

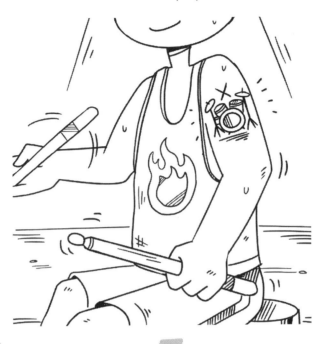

Why do you need to be careful around musical instruments?

Some are known for their sharpness.

What is a baker's favorite musical note?

Dough.

How do you express gratitude to the triangle player?

"Thank you for every ting."

Why did the retired boxer become a musician?

He wanted to make a hit.

Why did the burglar sing the song so poorly?

He broke in without the right key.

What did the musician order at the Kentucky Fried Chicken (KFC) restaurant?

Drumsticks.

How do two musicians become friends?

They strike a chord together.

Why don't sound techs get annual performance reviews?

They hate feedback.

Why did the stockbroker recommend that his client invest in musical instruments?

They are a sound investment.

Why did the music critic study lava in the past?

He liked rock even before it was cool.

What musical instrument is found in most household restrooms?

Tuba toothpaste.

What is the secret to having a great sounding guitar?

It is a secret . . . stay tuned.

What did the musician eat for Thanksgiving dinner?

Drumsticks.

Who are the most likable, well-rounded people in the music business?

The audio guys; they are sound guys.

What kind of music do jewelers prefer?

Rock.

What's the polite thing to reply when someone asks to sing a song with you?

"I'll duet."

How do rappers cheer?

"Hip Hop . . . Hooray!"

Which bone is the most musical?

The trom-bone.

Music

How much does a grand piano cost?

$1,000, of course.

What kind of salary did the baritone receive?

A bass salary.

What is a stepdad's favorite music?

Alternative pop.

What did the music teacher's ears suffer upon hearing a poor performance from his students?

It was A Minor injury.

Why do many musicians carry paper with them?

Because many of the tunes in their heads are noteworthy.

How is the collector of vinyl records like a secretary recording notes of a meeting?

Both are record keepers.

Why was the guitar so good with the blues?

It was constantly getting picked on.

Did you hear the joke about the broken horn?

It just didn't sound right.

Is it true the stereo system has a problem not in the subwoofer?

It's baseless.

Why is it hard to offer advice to electric guitar players?

They don't like feedback.

What did the career guidance counselor say when the graduate couldn't choose between mining coal and playing guitar?

"Take your pick."

What kind of guitar gets colds?

Achoo-stic.

How much money do piano builders make?

They make about a Grand a month.

Do you understand how smoke machines work at concerts?

I have a foggy idea.

Music

Try These Tongue Twisters

Helen's heart hopped hearing Henry's hurried harp hubbub.

Bubba's tube of Tuba Twinkle twinkled on Bubba's tuba tube.

Melody's memorized melody melded into many melodic music maestro's minds.

Careless Carol cared caroling carols.

Knock-Knock.

Who's there?
I'm Singing Solo.

I'm Singing Solo who?
I'm Singing Solo you can't hear me.

Knock-Knock.

Who's there?
Odd E.O.

Odd E.O. who?
Odd E.O. (audio) people are concerned with sound.

Knock-Knock.

Who's there?
Sarah Nader.

Sarah Nader who?
Sarah Nader is someone who sings songs outside your window at night.

Knock-Knock.

Who's there?
Disco.

Disco who?
Disco there; that go there.

Knock-Knock.

Who's there?
Opera Tune.

Opera Tune who?
Opera Tune time to hear some new jokes.

Knock-Knock.

Who's there?
D Minor, B Flat.

D Minor, B Flat who?
D Minor, B Flat because the mine car knocked him down.

Knock-Knock.

Who's there?
A Choir.

A Choir who?
A Choir (acquire) good grades, and lots of opportunities will open later in life.

Knock-Knock.

Who's there?
Benjamin.

Benjamin who?
Benjamin with all my friends, making beautiful music.

Knock-Knock.

Who's there?
Tooter.

Tooter who?
Tooter (tutor) will help you if you don't understand something at school.

Knock-Knock.

Who's there?
Polka.

Polka who?
Polka person in the ribs and they may get mad.

Knock-Knock.

Who's there?
Anna.

Anna who?
"Anna one, anna two, anna three . . ."

Knock-Knock.

Who's there?
Choir.

Choir who?
Choir eyes out at the sad movie; I brought tissue.

Chapter Fifteen:
Pirates

Ahoy, matey!

Shiver my timbers, are ye ready for some pirate jokes?

Well, I've searched the seven seas and have a treasure chest of jokes here. Let's see what they ar-r-r-r-r-r-r!

What happened when the pirate woke up and found his wooden leg was missing?

He was hopping mad.

What type of parties do pirates prefer?

Come as you arrrr parties.

How do pirates make sure they are in agreement with each other?

They try to see aye to aye.

Which pirate is in charge of marketing?

The sails manager.

Why are sword jokes hard to understand?

They often have duel meanings.

Why did the angry pirates exchange salutes?

It was an aye-for-an-aye.

Which pirate is the loudest of all the pirates?

The one who makes your earring.

What did the boy pirate focus on at school instead of the 3 R's?

The 7 C's.

What accessory does Apple make for pirates?

The iPatch.

What did the pirate in the jail cell tell his friend?

"Long time, no sea."

Why did the pirate carry a jump rope?

He was the ship's skipper.

What happened to the pirate who was trying to learn Spanish?

He got lost at "Si".

Why did the pirate go to the television newsroom?

He was in search of an anchor.

Which pirate is an eye doctor?

The sea captain.

What grades did the pirate get on his report card?

High C's.

Pirates

What vegetable did the pirate refuse to allow on the ship?

Leeks.

What do you call a pirate ship sailing in your belly button?

A naval boat.

What happens when a pirate gets excited about something?

He goes overboard.

What did the pirate captain say to his crew after they made a mess on the island?

"Cleanup needed on Isle One."

What did the gangplank say when the pirate ignored it?

"I'm board."

How do you know when a pirate ship has a quality gangplank?

It's board certified.

What did the pirate say as he hobbled through the snow on his wooden leg?

"Shiver me timber!"

Why do pirates carry swords?

Because swords can't move by themselves.

What did the pirate say when asked, "Is that land?"

"Shore."

What is a pirate's favorite pronoun?

"Aye."

What did the doctor say to the pirate?

"Open up and say "Arrrr'."

What did the pirate dressed as Santa Clause say to the children?

"Yo-Ho-Ho! Merry Christmas!"

What did the peg-leg pirate say when he stood too close to the campfire?

"Well, sizzle my timbers!"

Why was the pirate so bad at golf?

He had a left hook.

Pirates

What is the pirate's favorite shot to take in basketball?

The hook shot.

Why did the pirate go to the beach?

He wanted some Arr and Arr.

Why was the pirate sometimes seasick and sometimes not?

It came in waves.

Why did the pirate fail his alphabet test?

He thought there were seven C's.

What tool did the gardening pirate request from his assistant?

Land hoe

Why are pirates called pirates?

They just Arrrrrrrrrr!

Why did the pirate want to get into broadcasting?

He wanted to work with news anchors.

Why did the pirate break up with the girl on the nearby boat?

They had drifted apart.

How did the pirate captain introduce the gangplank to the crew?

"Welcome, a board."

What's the difference between a mistake made by an ordinary person and one made by a pirate?

To err is human; to arr is pirate.

Shiver me timbers! Why did the pirate go to Antarctica?

To find brrrrrr-ied treasure.

What is a pirate's favorite letter?

Some say it is "R" because the pirate says it all the time.
Others say it is "C" because he loves to sail the ocean. I've heard it is "P" because without "P", a "pirate" is simply "irate".

I think the letter the pirate likes to see most is "X" because "X" marks the spot where the treasure is.

"What is two in roman numerals?" the pirate captain asked his crew.

The crew replied, "Aye, Aye, Captain."

Pirates

Have you ever wondered where the tradition of pirates mumbling, "Arrrr" came from?

Here is one possible explanation: Once upon a time, there was a pirate captain who believed that pirates should speak the queen's English. One day, some of his crew members went into town and did not come back to the boat before curfew. The captain was furious. He took the first mate and walked into town to find them, scold them, and take them back to the boat.

As the captain and first mate walked along the busy street, the first mate saw the missing crew members, pointed to them, and stated, "There they be."

"Are," corrected the grammar-mind captain.

"Arrr," the first mate agreed, thinking this was how you expressed displeasure.

To this day, when a pirate is frustrated, angry, or otherwise cannot find the word to express his feelings, he resorts to "Arrr."

Try These Tongue Twisters

Sure, she sells Sam sails so Sam sails by seashells on the seashore.

I rate the irate pirate's eye rate.

The captain's capped tan captain's cap kept the captain tan.

Knock-Knock.

Who's there?
Ahoy, My Tea.

Ahoy, My Tea who?
Ahoy, My Tea. Welcome aboard.

Knock-Knock.

Who's there?
Captain.

Captain who?
Captain of the bottles and leave the other ten uncapped.

Knock-Knock.

Who's there?
Private Sea.

Private Sea who?
Private Sea (privacy) is a nice change if you have had people around you all day.

Knock-Knock.

Who's there?
I, Pat Chez.

I, Pat Chez who?
I, Pat Chez are what pirates wear when they have an eye injury.

Knock-Knock.

Who's there?
Cap N.

Cap N. who?
Cap N. of this ship says we'll have to walk the plank if we can't tell another joke.

Knock-Knock.

Who's there?
Wooden Leg.

Wooden Leg who?
Wooden Leg my brother go outside without a raincoat when I saw it was raining.

Knock-Knock.

Who's there?
Arr!

Arr! Who?
Arr! you ready for some more jokes?

Knock-Knock.

Who's there?
Arr!

Arr! Who?
Arr! class is going on a field trip this spring.

Pirates

Knock-Knock.

Who's there?
Treasure Chest.

Treasure Chest who?
Treasure Chest (chess); the reason to treasure it is because with its knights and castles, is a great game.

Knock-Knock.

Who's there?
Rosa Shore.

Rosa Shore who?
Rosa Shore and looks for treasure; that's what a pirate does.

Knock-Knock.

Who's there?
Rhoda.

Rhoda who?
"Rhoda boat to shore, my hardy! Yo-Ho-Ho!"

Knock-Knock.

Who's there?
French Ship.

French Ship who?
French Ship and friends are very special.

Chapter Sixteen:
School

For my great grandpa, school was simply going to class in a one-room rural schoolhouse. Today's school, though, is the classroom and so much more. We have sports teams, interest groups, cafeterias, and gymnasiums. Grandpa had one teacher who taught everyone, but we have lots of teachers. And principals – we can't forget about them.

My teachers make us trade papers to grade them. In that spirit, I am going to share my school jokes with you. I hope you'll give me an A.

How did the irritated teacher feel?

Testy.

Why was the student praised for supergluing herself to the school administrators?

She stuck to her principals.

Why was the principal suspicious of the art teacher?

Some of her classes were sketchy.

What should you do if somebody tells you they make straight A's?

Ask if their Bs, Cs, Ds, Es, Fs and Gs are straight too.

How do musicians study for a test?

They read their notes.

What did the school vending machine say when the coin got stuck in it?

"Money sure is tight these days."

School

How is a student taking a test like a camera taking a picture?

Both must stay focused.

Why did the boy quit writing the report after his pencil lead broke?

There was no point to continue.

Why did the boy not apply to the debate team?

He was talked out of it.

Are locksmiths and janitors important in a high school?

They are key workers.

What is the secret to addition?

Give it sum thought.

What is capital punishment?

When you get in trouble for writing in all capital letters.

Can knot-tying be learned?

"Knots" can be taut.

Why do homework in front of a mirror?

It helps you reflect.

What kind of tests do balloons hate the most?

Pop quizzes.

Why did the rowdy student read the theater textbook?

He wanted to get his act together.

Why did the student smear chocolate on his math test?

He wanted to fudge the numbers.

What subject at school counts the most?

Math, of course.

Why couldn't the chopped tree pass the quiz?

It got stumped.

Why should you stand while doing homework?

You have to think on your feet.

School

Why was the eraser so angry?

Someone rubbed him up the wrong way.

Why did the boy call the local pizza parlor when he needed help with his subtraction homework?

He heard they did takeaway.

Why are Siamese twins very wise?

Two heads are better than one.

What school supply can be talked into almost anything?

The pencil is easily lead.

Which school supply has no sense of humor?

The ruler is very straight forward.

Why did the students find it hard to fool the geometry teacher?

She knew all the angles.

Why are pencils kept sharp?

That's the point.

What must every student draw if he wants to get out of art class alive?

His breath.

Is teeter tottering (going on a seesaw) at recess fun?

It has its ups and downs.

Why doesn't the school library have any books on automatic transmission?

It just has manuals.

What are deadlines in weaving class called?

Looming deadlines.

Why are soccer players so smart in school?

They know how to use their heads.

Where do belly buttons go to school?

The navel academy.

Which school supplies are the rudest?

Scissors; they make cutting remarks.

School

What's the worst part of the art teacher's job when teaching students origami?

Lots of paperwork.

Why didn't the scissors announce candidacy for the election?

No one would run with them.

Was putting on the elementary school drama easy?

It was child's play.

Why didn't the boy get to tour the school library?

It was fully booked.

What's the king of the school supplies?

The ruler.

Where do surfers attend classes?

Boarding school.

What did the art student confess when he got in trouble?

"I guess I don't know where to draw the line."

Why was the girl in trouble when
she started to make paper dolls while waiting in line for lunch?

She was cutting in line.

How are teachers, charismatic preachers, and bank robbers alike?

They all want you to put up your hands.

How do you get
into marionette school?

You have to pull a few strings.

Did you hear about
the secret society of school librarians?

They keep it hush-hush.

Was the final project in the Home
Economics baking class easy?

It was a piece of cake.

Which teacher is known for their
decision-making skills?

The math teacher solves more problems
than any other teacher.

How did the substitute teacher
get to school?

The sub way.

Which teacher does not appreciate gifts?

The history teacher; he cares very little
for the present.

What happened when the history teacher wrote "History"
in cursive letters and then wrote it again in block letters?

The history teacher rewrote history.

School

Teacher: You are currently failing Ethics.

Student (puts a $20-bill on the teacher's desk):
How am I doing now?

∗ • • • ∗ • • • 🎖 • • • ∗ • • • ∗

One first grader confessed to another as they walked outside
on a spring day, "Bees scare me."

The other replied, "Bees scare me too.
In fact, the whole alphabet is scary to me."

"I didn't know what the ninth letter of the alphabet was,
but I took a guess, and I was right."

∗ • • • ∗ • • • 🎖 • • • ∗ • • • ∗

Try These Tongue Twisters

The teacher taught the tot to tie taut tot ties.
Teachers text tests to test tests over texts.

Spud spilt sparking soda so the soda spilt specifically
on his misspelled spelled spelling words.

Principal Paul politely paused prideful Polly's
policing of politics at Poly High.

Studious students started steadily studying studies of steadily
studying staring.

Knock-Knock.

Who's there?
Linda Book.

Linda Book who?
Linda Book to me please; I want to read something else later.

Knock-Knock.

Who's there?
Tess.

Tess who?
Tess are longer than quizzes; the teacher gives them to make sure we understand the material.

Knock-Knock.

Who's there?
Lesson.

Lesson who?
Lesson the amount of your television time if you feel like you are not understanding your schoolwork.

Knock-Knock.

Who's there?
L.E.

L.E. who?
L.E. -mentary school comes first, then middle school and high school.

Knock-Knock.

Who's there?
Kenny Reed.

Kenny Reed who?
Kenny Reed; reading is something everyone should learn.

Knock-Knock.

Who's there?
Thurston.

Thurston who?
Thurston (thirsting) for knowledge.

Knock-Knock.

Who's there?
ABC.

ABC who?
ABC person has things to do; I've got places to go and people to see.

Knock-Knock.

Who's there?
Honor Roll.

Honor Roll who?
Honor Roll (on a roll) I like to have some butter.

School

Knock-Knock.

Who's there?
Exam.

Exam who?
Exam (eggs, ham) and bacon are part of a complete breakfast.

Knock-Knock.

Who's there?
Miss Inga Page.

Miss Inga Page who?
**Miss Inga Page; I can't believe someone ripped
it out of my library book.**

Knock-Knock.

Who's there?
Library.

Library who?
Library little; always try to tell the truth and avoid lying.

Knock-Knock.

Who's there?
Overdue.

Overdue who?
Overdue (overdo) anything and you will be sore the next morning.

Knock-Knock.

Who's there?
Your Pencil.

Your Pencil who?
Your Pencil fall down to your ankles if you don't wear a belt.

Knock-Knock.

Who's there?
Wise.

Wise who?
Wise it so quiet in here?

Knock-Knock.

Who's there?
Hy Marx.

Hy Marx.
Hy Marx are the goal of most students who like school.

Knock-Knock.

Who's there?
Mr. Buss.

Mr. Buss who?
Mr. Buss; now you've got to walk to school.

Chapter Seventeen:
Space

The wild West of the United States, the Amazon jungle, the South Pole, and the heart of Africa have all been explored, although there is still much to learn about each of these. Today, space is considered the last frontier.

Will people journey to the moon for vacation in our generation? Will a human being walk on Mars? The answer may be no – or it could be yes. A lot of exciting discoveries have been made about space since the first satellite orbited the globe in the late 1950s – and there are still lots of discoveries to be made.

People often joke about what is on their minds, and therefore space jokes will likely remain popular for many generations to come. Here are some of the best space jokes on the planet - or any planet, for that matter.

What did the alien say to the cola upon meeting it?

Take me to your liter.

Space

What do astronauts use to keep warm in the rocket-ship?

Space heaters.

Are astronauts successful people?

Most go up in this world.

What happened when the astronaut on Mars found out he had won the lottery?

He was over the moon.

How exciting was the party in space?

It was out of this world.

What did the doctor diagnose when the astronaut could not remain focused?

He was spacey.

What did the astronaut say to Mission Control when he got his foot stuck in a wad of gum?

"Help! I am stuck in Orbit."

Why do astronauts blow their noses with such ease?

It's snot rocket science.

What is the most sought-after heavenly body in our universe?

The sun is the star.

Why did the greedy man want to go into space?

He had all the money in the world; he wanted all the money in space too.

Which celestial being wears a cape?

The Super Star.

What kind of alien gets right up in your face?

A space invader.

Why do astronauts have such big dreams of travelling to the moon?

Because they aren't down to earth.

Why did the astronaut name his rocket Bad News?

Bad News travels fast.

What did the teacher say when the student announced she wanted to be an astronaut when she grew up?

"I have high hopes for you too."

What do rocket scientists do on their day off?

What do you mean you don't know? It's not rocket science.

What happened when the cook threw a small plate like a frisbee and the U.F.O-believer saw it?

The U.F.O.-believer reported a flying saucer.

How do we know the astronaut was impressed with the moon?

He said it was out of this world.

Is gravity handsome?

It is very attractive.

How is Saturn like a circus?

Both have three rings.

Space

Which parent is more like the sun?

Dad; like father, like sun.

Why don't more people believe there is life on other planets?

It's an alien concept.

What did the alien say to the clerk at the garden center?

"Take me to your cedar."

What did the carpenter say to convince everyone that he had seen a space alien?

"I know what I saw."

What did the alien say to the painter?

"Take me to your ladder."

How is the sun like a diva?

Everything revolves around it.

Why are Martians such great gardeners?

They have green thumbs.

What is the unit of measurement for a space rock?

A meteor (and we use a meteor stick to measure it).

How are ocean waves like unmarried men?

The mood affects the tide and the untied.

Why did the astronaut wear a bullet-proof vest?

To protect himself from any shooting stars.

What happened to the busy astronauts in the space lab?

They were "highly" productive.

Why wasn't the astronaut more serious about his studies?

He didn't understand the gravity of the situation.

Is gravity influential?

It has a lot of pull.

How is the otter's home like a rocket ship?

One is for otter space and the other for outer space.

Space

How did the Martian feel after landing on earth?

Alienated.

Have you heard predictions about the field of astronomy?

The astronomer's business is looking up.

What did the alien say to the cat?

"Take me to your litter."

Try These Tongue Twisters

Randy read red wet wind-up rockets wobble and rock wide rightward.

The count counted countdown.

The astronauts ate a round of round Altoids as asteroids ambled around the air around them.

Knock-Knock.

Who's there?
Apollo Guys.

Apollo Guys who?
Apollo Guys and say you are sorry if you do something to hurt someone's feelings.

Knock-Knock.

Who's there?
Martian.

Martian who?
Martian to the beat of my own drum.

Knock-Knock.

Who's there?
Jim and I.

Jim and I who?
Jim and I (Gemini) is one of the constellations which make up the zodiac.

Knock-Knock.

Who's there?
Sirius.

Sirius who?
Sirius about learning my constellations.

Knock-Knock.

Who's there?
Cancer.

Cancer who?
Can sir or madam help me get my shoe on?

Knock-Knock.

Who's there?
Rocket.

Rocket who?
Rocket to sleep if the baby cries.

Knock-Knock.

Who's there?
Cosmos.

Cosmos who?
Cosmos people to laugh when we share these jokes.

Knock-Knock.

Who's there?
Neptune.

Neptune who?
Neptune (nap tune) will help put me to sleep.

Space

Knock-Knock.

Who's there?
Planet.

Planet who?
Planet and do it.

Knock-Knock.

Who's there?
Alien.

Alien who?
Alien the morning, I get up, wash up, and get ready for school.

Knock-Knock.

Who's there?
Martian Orders.

Martian Orders who?
Martian Orders are what the generals give to the troops.

Chapter Eighteen:
Sports

I love playing American football in the backyard. I am a tall person, so on a third down and short yardage situation, I am usually given the ball and asked to stretch out as I get tackled; because of my long reach, I can usually get a first down.

Whether you like American football, soccer (football to the rest of the world), baseball, hockey or basketball, there are jokes about your sport. Most of us like to joke as we play; it makes a fun time even more fun.

Do you know how the treadmill testing went?

The tester didn't get anywhere.

Why are baby cows such great runners?

They use their calf muscles.

Which cereal exercises at the gym?

Corn flex.

Why don't vegetarians participate in swim competitions?

They don't like meats.

How is a baseball team like a birthday cake?

Both depend on good batters.

How dedicated do you have to be to win at limbo?

You have to be willing to bend over backwards.

Sports

How do karate instructors greet their friends?

"Hi, ya."

Why did the square and the triangle
go to the gym?

To stay in shape.

Why do bowling pins tell jokes?

So they can fall down laughing.

Why did the baseball team recruit
the fast-food burger cook?

He could make singles, doubles,
and triples.

What sport is popular in Alabama,
Mississippi, and Mexico?

The golf of Mexico.

Why couldn't the baseball concession
stand get cans open?

The day of the doubleheader, the home
team had lost the opener.

What's so unique about
a tennis ball?

It's about the only place you'll see tennis
players dance.

Why did the boxer not wear glasses?

Because boxing is a contact sport.

What did the clumsy but optimistic baseball player believe?

"If at first you don't succeed, try second."

What's the nose's favorite sport?

It likes to run.

Is yo-yoing fun?

It has its ups and downs.

Did you hear about the American marathon runner who ran for three hours but only moved two feet?

They were the only feet he had.

What happened when the trainer couldn't lift a fifty-pound weight?

He had to put in his too weak notice.

Why did the bench presser see a counselor?

He had things he wanted to get off his chest.

Sports

Why is bungee jumping
so expensive?

It's not a freefall.

What do you wear if you do not want
to dress like a winner, but you also don't
want to look like a loser?

A tie.

What do you call the excitement
generated by a sailboat race?

Mast hysteria.

Why does the ballet dancer celebrate
February second each year?

It's 2/2.

Why can't you trust
a softball pitcher?

She has underhanded techniques.

What's better than getting on the
treadmill for 30 minutes today?

Actually turning it on.

Why did the basketball player refuse
to go on a cruise ship?

His coach said he traveled too much.

Why did the doctor tell the man
to run the marathon rather than
the 100-yard dash?

He thought he'd be better off
in the long run.

What do you call an estimate of a
stadium's size?

A ballpark figure.

What's one thing everyone should
exercise at the gym?

Caution.

Was the basketball excited about
the big game?

Yes. It was pumped.

Why did Junior refuse to be the goalie
on his brother's soccer team?

He didn't want to be his brother's keeper.

How did the athlete smell having not taken a shower for days?

Through his nose.

What is the scariest of all sports injuries?

The boooooo-boooooo.

How did the pool player get famous?

He got a big break.

What kind of exercise is the river addicted to doing?

The river won't stop running.

Which sports ball is the cutest?

The golf ball; it has dimples.

What did the basketball player say to make a promise?

"Cross my heart and hoop to die."

How do you know that bowling players are prepared?

When they are ready to roll.

Sports

What did the waiter say to the tennis ball?

Have you been served yet?

What did the bored bowler do?

He split.

What happens if you don't exercise for seven days straight?

Seven days makes one weak.

What did the second-string baseball player say to the flight attendant when she asked him what his seat preference was?

"Put me in coach."

With runners on first and second bases, why did the baseball coach send the dog up to bat?

Dogs are usually walked at least twice each day.

Which member of the baseball team distributed the lemonade?

The pitcher.

In which sport/recreational activity must you be alert?

In ballet; ballerinas must be on their toes.

Why did the billiards player take so long to take a shot?

He was waiting for his cue.

What four letter-sport begins with a "t"?

Golf. (I hope you found this joke up to par.)

What is the easiest sport to enter?

I heard limbo is; they are known for having the bar set very low.

Why was the opera singer so good at baseball?

He had a perfect pitch.

Why did the dieter go to the paint store instead of the gym?

She heard you could get thinner there.

Why isn't sunbathing an Olympic sport?

Participants are only interested in getting bronze.

Was the coach happy with the runner's improvement?

Yes; he said she was making great strides.

Sports

What do retired golfers do?

Putter around.

The athlete had just tied his gym shoes and was preparing to go for a run.

The shoe looked up at the laces and said, "Can you relax a little? You're awfully tight."

The laces replied, "I'd rather knot."

Boy: Dad, I just watched a man do 100 pushups. Can you do that?

Dad: Of course. What kind of man would I be otherwise?
I can even watch people do many more than 100."

I am not sure how you score a ballet,
but I heard someone say something about 2-2.

Try These Tongue Twisters

The quarter's quite quiet, quiet fans quit questioning being quite quiet.

Billy Bob bobbled then bounded Bill Bright's bright basketball beautifully.

Hockey hackers hocked hacked hokey hockey helmets.

Football fans found free footballs on Football Fan Night.

The Tut-Tut Tutu tutu took two Tut-Tut Tutu teams to throw together today.

Knock-Knock.

Who's there?
A Tourney.

A Tourney who?
A Tourney is a lawyer.

Knock-Knock.

Who's there?
Quarterback.

Quarterback who?
Quarterback is what you get when you give 25 cents too much to the cashier.

Knock-Knock.

Who's there?
Dumbbell.

Dumbbell who?
Dumbbell on your door doesn't work so I had to knock.

Knock-Knock.

Who's there?
Jim Shuse.

Jim Shuse who?
Jim Shuse are important if you are going to play on the gym floor.

Knock-Knock.

Who's there?
Lee Ping.

Lee Ping who?
Lee Ping often requires a running start.

Knock-Knock.

Who's there?
Gladiator.

Gladiator who?
Gladiator fries before she threw them away.

Knock-Knock.

Who's there?
I won.

I won who?
I won to tell you more jokes; do you want to hear them?

Knock-Knock.

Who's there?
Hockey.

Hockey who?
Hockey (her key) should unlock the locker.

Sports

Knock-Knock.

Who's there?
Badminton.

Badminton who?
Badminton is a mitten with holes in the fingers.

Knock-Knock.

Who's there?
Relay.

Relay who?
Relay, really like telling knock-knock jokes with you.

Knock-Knock.

Who's there?
Archery.

Archery who?
Archery jam was one of the best cherry jams at the county canning festival.

Chapter Nineteen:
Vacation

Have you been on a vacation recently? I went camping once and slept out in a tent. That may be your idea of fun but give me a hotel over a tent any day. At the hotel, they have soft comfortable beds – and I don't have to make my bed since a maid is coming. I love racing my sister to the ice-machine and going swimming in the pool.

Everybody needs a vacation. Even if you can't travel, these hotel jokes will give you a break from daily life.

What type of ghosts investigate crimes in hotels?

Inn specters.

What does a glutton do on vacation?

Checks out hotel sweets.

Why is waking up sometimes such a shock?

It's an eye-opening experience.

Vacation

What happened to the boy who kicked off his blankets in his sleep?

He recovered.

When the hotel guest asked for an early morning wake-up call, what did the receptionist say?

"What are you doing with your life?"

If you can't get good Internet connections in your hotel room, what should you do?

Go to the lobby; they have reception there.

Why didn't the hotel bed have a Valentine's date?

The hotel maid kept turning it down.

Are hotel jokes popular?

Yes. They are very inn.

Why was the hotel staffed by Southern girls with noise makers so expensive?

It had all the belles and whistles.

Why was the meeting room so quiet?

It was reserved.

Why was the hotel guest so nervous?

This was her last resort.

A man approached the hotel desk clerk and stated,
"I'd like a room for the night, please."

The desk clerk looked up and asked,
"Do you have reservations?"

"Yes," the man replied,
"However, my wife wants to stay here anyway."

Try These Tongue Twisters

Holly's holiday hotel had holiday holly held for Holly's holiday.

Victor and Valerie Vicker's valley vacation valet very vigorously voiced a veto when Valerie and Victor Vicker voted varying valets.

Limber Larry lifted and lugged lovely Lori's luggage of luxury linens.

Knock-Knock.

Who's there?
Lodge.

Lodge who?
Lodge, medium, or small – we have souvenir t-shirts in all sizes.

Knock-Knock.

Who's there?
Inn.

Inn who?
"In" is the opposite of "out".

Vacation

Knock-Knock.

Who's there?
Rock Inn.

Rock Inn who?
Rock Inn and a rolling.

Knock-Knock.

Who's there?
Moe Tell.

Moe Tell who?
Moe Tell is similar to a hotel but not quite as fancy.

Knock-Knock.

Who's there?
Chicken.

Chicken who?
Chicken is any time after 3 p.m. and checkout is at noon.

Knock-Knock.

Who's there?
Arrival.

Arrival who?
A rival who wants the same things you want.

Knock-Knock.

Who's there?
Inn Appropriate.

Inn Appropriate who?
Inn Appropriate language is not tolerated by my parents.

Knock-Knock.

Who's there?
Tucker Inn.

Tucker Inn who?
Tucker Inn every night when she goes to sleep.

Knock-Knock.

Who's there?
Roomer.

Roomer who?
Roomer (rumor) you were eating dessert before your meal; is that true?

Knock-Knock.

Who's there?
Hostel.

Hostel who?
Hostel (hostile) people get mad easily.

Knock-Knock.

Who's there?
Vile Inns.

Vile Inns who?
Vile Inns make beautiful music.

Knock-Knock.

Who's there?
The Czech Inn.

The Czech Inn who?
The Czech Inn time is any time after 3 p.m.

Knock-Knock.

Who's there?
Boarder.

Boarder who?
Boarder separates the United States from Canada.

Knock-Knock.

Who's there?
Guest.

Guest who?
Guest how many jellybeans were in the jar and won a prize at the carnival.

Chapter Twenty:
The Kitchen Sink

When people say, "It has everything; it even has the kitchen sink", they mean that something is complete. No good joke book is complete, then, without a couple of jokes about – what else? – the kitchen sink.

Plumbers are special people. We may not see them on a regular basis, but when we do see them it is always an eventful occasion. At our house, we had a night when the shower wouldn't shut off and was filling up the bathtub so fast we were afraid it was going to flood the house. Even when the visit is more routine, such as replacing a hot water heater, fixing a leaking sink, or clearing a clogged toilet, my mom and dad always seem stressed when they call a plumber. Here are some plumber jokes to help lighten the mood and to remember those past times.

Should you stop to ponder what's happening if you are playing video games and the hardware store personnel knocks on the door to deliver a new kitchen sink?

Yes; pause to let that sink in.

How do you make a kitchen sink?

Dump the kitchen into the ocean.

What do you tell noisy plumbers?

Pipe down.

How do plumbers knock?

With a tap.

Why was the plumber sad?

His career was in the toilet.

What happened when the dirty dishes began to sing in harmony?

They were in sink.

What kind of injury did the plumber get working on the toilet?

A flush wound.

How do you describe people who have never tried city water?

Well hydrated.

Why are plumbers so dedicated?

They take doody seriously.

Why did the faucet stop working?

It tapped out.

Why did the plumber go to the opera?

He liked good pipes wherever they were found.

Why did the plumber go to the orchard?

Someone said they needed a plummer.

The Kitchen Sink

Why was the plumber hired by the news media?

To find where the leaks were.

What type of dance do plumbers like to watch?

Tap dance.

What is scary about a bathtub?

Sometimes when you lean back near the spout, you can feel a tap on your shoulder.

How do plumbers like their coffee?

Piping hot.

Why did the ditch-digging plumber want to change careers?

He thought he was in a rut.

What's required to stare intently at a pipe that is wide at the top and narrow at the bottom?

Funnel vision.

Why did the plumber retire?

His career went down the drain.

Do all the plumbers' wishes come true?

No; some are pipe dreams.

What vegetables do plumbers seek to put an end to?

Leeks.

What happened when the plumber lost the wrestling match?

He tapped out.

Why did Mom not let Junior hang around the plumber?

The plumber had a potty mouth.

Why did the plumber quit his job?

It was very draining.

What kind of dancing does a plumber do best?

Tap dancing.

Why was the plumber's assistant being extra careful?

When he climbed under the sink, the plumber called, "Be careful; it's a trap."

What kind of dancing shoes are the plumber's favorite?
(Hint: It's not tap shoes.)

Clogs.

What happened once the plumber worked up his nerve to fix the plugged toilet?

He took the plunge.

What did the customer sigh when the plumber got the faucet unclogged?

"Water relief."

The Kitchen Sink

Try These Tongue Twisters

The plum plump plum was the plump plumber's plum.

The plumber's plunger plunged plenty of unpleasant plugged places.

Kat's kitchen cat kept Kat's cat's kittens company catching Kat's car kits in the kitchen.

Knock-Knock.

Who's there?
Yurri Nal.

Yurri Nal who?
Yurri Nal is a standard feature in men's restrooms.

Knock-Knock.

Who's there?
Lee King.

Lee King who?
Lee King faucets keep plumbers in business.

Knock-Knock.

Who's there?
Duane Pipes.

Duane Pipes who?
Duane Pipes, remove the crud stuck in them, and then put them back.

Did you enjoy the book?

If you did, we are ecstatic. If not, please write your complaint to us and we will ensure we fix it.

If you're feeling generous, there is something important that you can help me with —
tell other people that you enjoyed the book.

Ask a grown-up to write about it on Amazon.
When they do, more people will find out about the book.
It also lets Amazon know that we are making kids around the world laugh. Even a few words and ratings would go a long way.

If you have any ideas or jokes that you think are super funny, please let us know. We would love to hear from you.

Riddleland Bonus

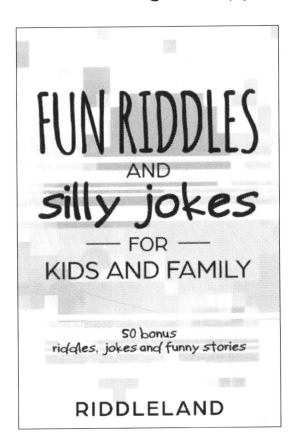

Join our **Facebook Group** at **Riddleland for Kids**
to get daily jokes and riddles.

https://pixelfy.me/riddlelandbonus

Thank you for buying this book. As a token of our appreciation,
we would like to offer a special bonus—a collection
of 50 original jokes, riddles, and funny stories.

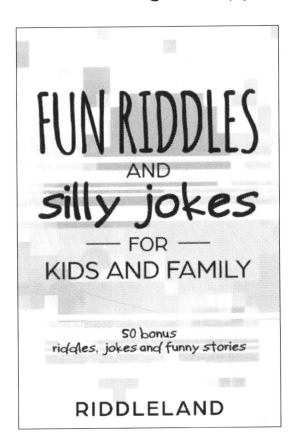

Other Fun Books By Riddleland

Riddles Series

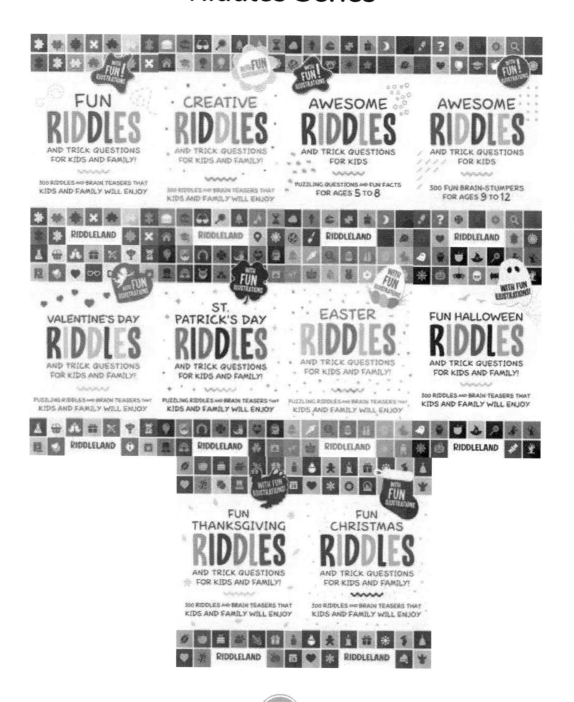

It's Laugh O'Clock Joke Books

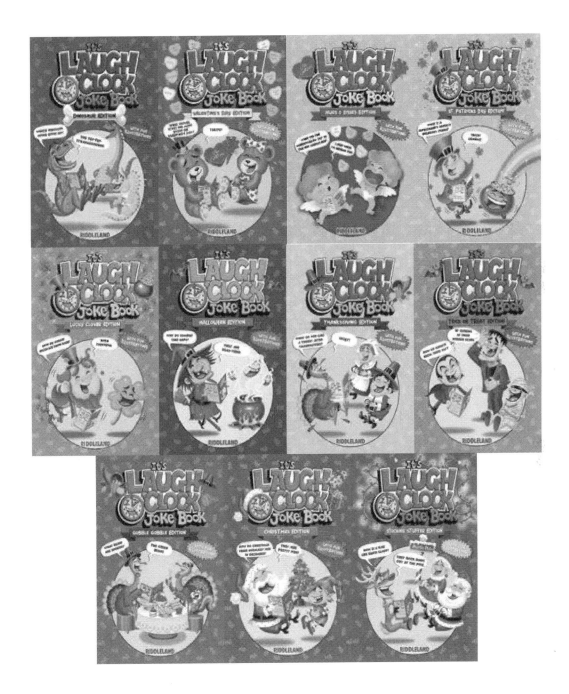

It's Laugh O'Clock Would You Rather Books

Get them on Amazon or our website at
www.riddlelandforkids.com

About Riddleland

Riddleland is a mum + dad run publishing company. We are passionate about creating fun and innovative books to help children develop their reading skills and fall in love with reading. If you have suggestions for us or want to work with us, shoot us an email at

riddleland@riddlelandforkids.com

Our family's favorite quote:

*"Creativity is an area in which younger people have
a tremendous advantage since they have
an endearing habit of always questioning
past wisdom and authority."*

~ Bill Hewlett